Practical Music Theory

James Lincoln Collier

Practical Music Theory

*How Music Is Put Together
from Bach to Rock*

W · W · NORTON & COMPANY · INC · New York

For Geoff, Dore, Jake, and Ryno—
whose ignorance made this book necessary.

Contents

Practical Music Theory

1

What Is Music?

WHAT IS MUSIC THEORY? Why study it? Why does anyone need to know it? Who has the right to say what is good music, and what is bad? Why not just depend on your ear to tell you the difference?

The answer is: of course, no matter what the rules say, the ear is the final judge of music.

Then why have rules? The answer to that question is this. Music theory is not a set of hard and fast rules for how music ought to be written and played. It is, rather, a way of thinking about music that helps composers and musicians to understand how it works. Music is made up of an almost infinite number of different sounds, rhythms, pitches, tone colors. You can, if you like, simply grab up a group of sounds at random and throw them together helter-skelter. And, as a matter of fact, some modern composers, like John Cage, have tried to do something rather like that. But most people don't find the end result very pleasing. For most of us, musical sounds need to be organized in some way before they mean anything to us.

Theory is a way of organizing the enormous number of sounds

1

possible in music. It shows us ways of combining sounds to get certain effects. And it changes. Over the long history of music, new theories—new ways of putting sounds together—have constantly arisen, usually springing out of the ones that came before. Some day the system of theory you are going to read about in this book will also be replaced by new ideas. There are other systems in use, but the one we will talk about seems likely to be used for a long while yet. Good music theory lives long, and dies hard, and the one we have today is a good one. It is more than three hundred years old, and although it has changed in many minor ways over that long span of time, it is still essentially the same as it was in 1600.

Virtually all of the music with which you are most familiar is built on this same theory: jazz, rock, folk music, classical music, popular music, movie music, and almost anything else you care to name. There are differences, of course, between these types of music, but underneath them all is one basic system of organizing musical tones. The answer to why you should study the theory of music, then, is that it will explain to you how the music around you is put together, so that you can play it better and enjoy it more when you hear it. Once you begin to grasp this theory, this way of organizing musical sound, you will have acquired several valuable tools. For one, you will be able to judge in advance fairly well what a given combination of notes sounds like: highly trained musicians can read a musical score the way you read a book, actually hearing in their heads what they see on paper. For another, as you rummage around in theory, it will suggest to you musical experiments to make: if you can build a chord on 3rds, why not on 4ths? If you can divide an octave into twelve parts, why not into twenty-four parts? For a third, you will be able to learn new pieces of music much more easily if you know theory: as you work your way through this book, you will learn to figure out fairly quickly the melody and chords of a new rock tune or pop song. And finally, knowing how music works will simply make music more pleasurable for you to listen to: [at the very least, it will make you feel superior to the clods around you who don't hear the difference between a dominant 7th and a flatted 5th.] \o\

Musicians learn music theory for the same reasons that contractors learn the rules of construction. A contractor can build any kind of house he wants, but it won't stay up unless he pays attention to all the rules of house building. And herein lies perhaps the most important reason for studying theory. Many contractors build houses without the help of architects, by using common sense and by figuring out the rules for themselves. In the same way you could undoubtedly work out a good deal of the basic theory of music for yourself, by listening and experimenting. But it would take you years to do it. After all, man has spent fifteen hundred years developing the theory we use today. Far better to simply learn it and then go on from there.

The discussion of theory you find in this book is by no means the end of the subject. There are all sorts of advanced aspects to it, like counterpoint, atonal music, and the musics of Asia and of Africa, which are built on entirely different theories. However, there is enough theory here with which you can begin. If you master this book—and there is no reason why you shouldn't be able to—you will be quite prepared to compose or arrange most of the kinds of music you normally hear. There is enough theory here, in fact, to write an entire symphony.

I seriously suggest that you don't try to read this book through at one sitting. It would be a far better idea to take it slowly, over several weeks, going over each chapter again and again until you understand it thoroughly and have the important points stuck firmly in your mind. In the back of this book I have put exercises to go with each chapter. Doing exercises can be a bore, but it is a good way to make sure that you understand what the chapter is about. Perhaps more important, they will help you develop some skill at taking music apart and putting it together again—which is, after all, what theory should teach you to do.

It might be helpful to go through this book with a friend. The more you discuss what you are learning with somebody, the better it will stick with you.

The best way to see if you understand something is to try to explain it to somebody. And you absolutely must understand each part as you go along. Music theory is like mathematics: everything is built upon something else. If you don't understand what goes before, you can't possibly understand what comes after.

Now, it is important to remember that music is not words or notes on paper, but sounds in the air. I have put in this book music illustrations of the points I am making. It is very important that you hear them. They are all quite simple. If you can sight-read vocal music or have studied an instrument for a few months, you will be able to play the scales and melodies I have put in. The chords are another problem. Ideally, the notes of a chord should be played all at once on a guitar, piano, organ, or other keyboard instrument. However, if you play some other instrument you can hear the effect almost as well if you play the chords one note at a time, starting from the bottom:

can be played like this:

However, since most of these examples are so simple, you can probably pick them out on the keyboard for yourself, even if you have never studied piano. If you look at a piano, you can see that the black notes are grouped in twos and threes. The white note just before each group of two black notes is a C:

The other white notes go on upwards along the alphabet: C, D, E, F, G, A, B, C, as you know, so that:

is played like this:

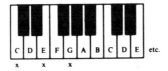

The Musical Tone

Now, what is music? Just as painting is an arrangement of space, so music is an arrangement of time. It is a series of patterns scrawled in the air, constantly shifting, changing, and disappearing as rapidly as they come. These patterns in the air, however, are not random, like falling snow or blowing mist. As I have said, music is an organization of sound. The mind automatically begins searching for patterns, for organizations, in anything it comes upon. If it fails to find these patterns in music, it usually turns away in boredom.

The basic building block of these musical patterns is the note, or tone, as we usually call it. A musical tone has four main qualities: length; loudness or softness; color, that is, whether it's a violin sound, a trumpet sound, and so forth; and pitch. (Actually, a tone has a good many other subtle qualities, too: how sharply it is begun and ended, whether it wavers, and other more complex matters; but we needn't worry about them now.) In this book I am not going to discuss tone color or loudness and softness. The length of a note is part of the subject of rhythm, which I will get into briefly later on. What we are mainly concerned with—and what music theory is mainly about—is pitch, and how groups of pitches can be organized.

What, then, is pitch? A musical sound is nothing more or less than a pulsation in the air, and a musical instrument is nothing more than a machine for creating these pulsations. A guitar string is plucked and vibrates for a brief moment; a clarinet is blown, and the reed begins to dance rapidly back and forth. Each time the string or reed moves back and forth, it gives the air particles around it a little punch. These particles bump the ones next to them, and in this fashion that little punch is carried through the air, like the rings going out from a stone dropped in water. If you want to test the effect, line up a half dozen marbles or so in a track or something equally convenient, so that they are touching tight together. Tap one end lightly: most of the marbles will stay more or less in place, but your tap will be carried down the line, and the marble at the other end will roll away.

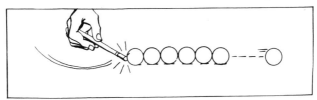

These tiny, rapid nudges move through the air until they begin bouncing against your eardrum, setting it vibrating. And the brain, in its miraculous fashion, turns the vibrations of your eardrum into sounds. (Just to give you an idea of how small these nudges in the air are, ordinary sounds move each air particle about one hundred-thousandth of an inch.)

All sound works this way. The difference between musical tones and other sounds is that the vibrations which make a tone are regular. That is, those little punches in the air are spaced out equally, each one coming along exactly the same fraction of a second behind the rest. Nonmusical sounds are merely a jumble of vibrations with no easily discernible pattern to them.

Octaves

The number of vibrations a pitch has per second is called its frequency. The human ear can hear pitches of frequencies ranging from about 20 per second to 20,000 per second, depending on the sensitivity of a person's ear. The A above middle C on the piano vibrates at a frequency of 440. There is no law of nature establishing the 440 A. We have simply agreed on it for convenience's sake. In the past, different frequencies have been used for this note—or I suppose I should say that different tones have been called A.

Now here is a key fact: every note vibrates exactly twice as fast as the note an octave below it. The note an octave above the 440 A vibrates at a frequency of 880; the note an octave below the 440 A has a frequency of exactly 220. And so it goes through the whole range of notes: go up an octave and you double the frequency.

Actually, we ought to put it the other way around. For a long period of time, man has recognized that certain notes seemed to be somehow "the same," even though one was higher than the other. In the beginning, he didn't know the frequency of A, or even what frequency was, but his ear told him it was very similar to all the other A's—in the same way that he could see that a big square and a little square were somehow "the same."

There are very good scientific reasons for our sensing notes an octave apart as being similar—quite fascinating if you like science, but the subject of the physics of sound is too complicated to study here. Let us just say that the idea of the octave has played an important part in every type of music we know about. We feel that if we play a scale of notes up and down, when we reach the octave we have begun to repeat ourselves.

Scales

This concept of the octave, then, immediately gives us a beginning to our organization of tones. Now, what about the notes between any given pair of octave notes?

Let's take the 440 A and the 220 A an octave below it. You can fit hundreds of tones in between these two A's—one at a frequency of 221, then 222, or even 222.5, or 222.00001. Theoretically, the number of notes between the two A's is infinite. But that's only theoretically. In actual fact, a trained ear can distinguish only about a hundred different pitches between the octaves; most untrained people can't distinguish more than fifty, if that many.

In many types of music, especially ones from Asia, octaves are divided into perhaps twenty-five or so pitches. In our Western music (the term covers the music of Europe and the Americas), we have come to settle on a division of the octave into twelve pitches—thirteen, if you count the octaves at both ends. We call these pitches half tones, because they are what we call "a half step" apart.

Taken together, the half tones in an octave make up what we call a chromatic scale. You can play a chromatic scale by starting at any point on the piano and playing thirteen successive black and white keys. A chromatic scale beginning on A looks like this:

Diatonic Scales

This division of the octave into twelve steps, however, is not the one you are most familiar with. There are other divisions which make use of whole steps. A whole step is two half-steps. In the chromatic scale, if you move from A to A♯ you have moved a half step. If you move from A♯ to B you have moved another half step. But if you move from A to B, you have moved two half-steps—or a whole step. A jump from A to B, then, is a whole step.

The scale—the division of the octave with which you are most familiar—is made up of six whole-steps and two half-steps. It is the good old "do, re, mi" scale that you learned in kindergarten.

The "do, re, mi" scale is one of several scales made up of combinations of half and whole steps. They are called "diatonic" scales. They have eight steps, or tones, counting the octaves at the end—six whole-steps and two half-steps. The diatonic scales were invented by man hundreds of years ago, long before he had really worked out the chromatic scale. Consequently, he built his music and his theory on diatonic scales.

Obviously, there are a number of different ways to arrange two half-steps and six whole-steps. Over a period of time men have made up different arrangements to create different diatonic scales. Today, however, virtually all of the music you ordinarily hear is built up out of two diatonic scales called the major and minor scales. The most important of the two is the major scale. The cornerstone of Bach, rock, jazz, folk, pop tunes, and nursery-school songs is the major scale. And that is the good old do, re, mi.

The key point, which you absolutely must memorize, is that in the major scale the half steps are between the third note and the fourth, and between the seventh note and the eighth:

The minor scale is a little more complicated. It comes in three versions which are used for different purposes. Later on we will see what those uses are, but now I will mention only the natural minor, which has half steps between the second and third notes, and between the fifth and sixth notes:

But these are not the only ways you can arrange combinations of half steps and whole steps. Here are some other scales which you have sometimes heard without realizing it. The Dorian scale (usually called the Dorian mode) is used a good deal in rock and, to a lesser extent, in jazz:

The "Hungarian" scale was used by composers to imitate the sound of Slavic folk music:

The whole-tone scale has no half steps, and only seven notes, and can be heard in such music as Debussy's *The Sunken Cathedral.*

Composers today like to experiment with different scales, especially with a group called "modes," and you can have fun doing it yourself. But most of the music you know is based on major and minor scales—so much so that theorists often say that our Western music is based on a "major-minor system."

Sharps and Flats

As you have noticed, I started all the scales in these examples on C: they are all C scales. But you can begin a scale on any note —on D, or G, or B♭, or any of the others up and down the chromatic scale. All you have to do is make sure the half steps fall in the right place for the scale you want. Any time you put together a scale with a half step between the third and fourth notes and another between the seventh and eighth notes, you will have a major scale, no matter what the first note is (provided, of course, that the other steps are all whole steps).

Now, if you think about it for a minute, you will see that you can move the half steps around simply by putting sharps and flats in the right places. For example, let's take a C scale:

Now let's start it on F instead of C:

The new scale now has a half step between the seventh note and the eighth, which is correct for a major scale; but the other half step falls between the fourth and fifth notes, which is not correct. But if we add a flat in the right place, we get:

The half steps are now in the right place for an F-major scale.

And here, of course, is the explanation for key signatures—the sharps and flats at the beginning of pieces of music which seem such an unnecessary nuisance to beginning players. The function of the key signature is to set the half steps in the right place for the scale around which the composer wants to build his piece. And, of course, it is much simpler to put the sharps and flats at the beginning of each piece, rather than to have to keep putting them in all the way through. Scales must have something to do with keys, then; and in the next chapter we will see what.

2

Tonality and Intervals

MUSIC THEORY, as I said in the last chapter, is a way of organizing tones into groups and patterns that will make some sort of sense and have some sort of musical "meaning"—whatever "meaning" means. Already we have begun to put some of these patterns together. For one thing, we have discovered the octave, which helps to cut the huge range of possible tones into convenient sections. For another, we have found out how to make scales, which gives us groups or sets of notes which go together. Any note will fit into seven different major and seven different natural-minor scales (as well as seven "Hungarian" scales, six whole-tone scales, etc.) Thus, given any note, you can quickly find a number of other notes to which you can relate it.

This process of finding which notes go best with other notes is basic to music theory. It is, in fact, almost the whole idea of it. In theory we are always asking: What notes belong to the same sets? What notes will best fit in with some we already have? How do certain notes relate to others—that is, what makes them go together?

How, then, do the notes of a scale relate to one another?

Tonality

There is a note in every scale which seems more important than the rest. If you play notes at random out of a major scale, after a while you will find yourself returning to one note more frequently than to others. You find also that this note tends to sound final—like an ending. Until you get there the music seems slightly restless, unsatisfied, like a bird looking for a place to light. Then, when you reach it you get a feeling of relaxation, of having gotten home at last.

This note, the most important in the scale, is called the *tonic,* because it is the most important *tone.* The tonic in any scale is the first note. In a C-major scale the tonic is C. In a B♭-minor scale, the tonic is B♭. In an F♯-minor scale the tonic is F♯. And so forth.

This whole idea of each scale having an important "home" note is called tonality. But tonality does not apply only to scales: it applies to the songs that are made up out of them, too. That is, virtually every piece of music emphasizes certain notes. If these notes are mainly from an F scale, the music will seem to want very much to return to F often and to land on F when it finishes. Every scale has its home note, its tonic. Music made up from a scale has the same tonic as the scale.

This idea of tonality is basic to nearly all Western music, be it pop, rock, or Bach. Listen to any song, and you will find the notes of the melody tending to circle around the tonic, first darting away from it, then returning to it.

This explains what we mean when we talk about the "key" a song is in. The key tells us on what scale the song is built, and what its tonality is. And the key signature at the beginning of a piece is made up of the sharps or flats which set the half steps in the right places for that particular key.

Tonality, scale, key, tonic note: they aren't all the same, but they are distinctly related. A piece of music in the key of G major is built on a G-major scale. Its tonality is G, and its tonic—the home note to which the melody keeps returning—is G.

But what about the fact that you can begin a number of scales from the same tonic note? That is, beginning on, say, D, you can make a D-major scale, a D-minor scale, a D-Dorian scale, and so forth. The tonics of all these scales are the same, but the scales are different. What happens to the key signatures and the tonalities?

For now, forget about all scales but the major and minor. Since they are the basis of most of the music you hear, we will concentrate on them throughout this book. Now, you can make a major and a minor scale on any tonic. But since their half steps fall in different places, their key signatures must be different. Thus, every major key has a brother minor key with the same tonality but with a different scale and a different key signature. The minor key has three more flats, or three fewer sharps than its major brother:

F Major   F Minor   E Major   E Minor

Sometimes you have to subtract sharps and add flats, but you will come out right if they total up to three:

G Major   G Minor

Each major key, thus, has what we call its tonic minor, and vice versa. These pairs are keys with the same tonic, but different scales. But there is another way to play this game, for if we look, we can find pairs of keys with the same *scale*, but different *tonics*. These are called relative keys. Each major has its relative minor with the same key signature, the same scale, but a different tonic:

B♭ Major   G Minor

Both B♭-major and G-minor scales need two flats to set the half steps where they belong; both, then, will have the same key signature—two flats. So each key has two brothers: one with the same tonic, and one with the same scale. This information will be most useful to you a little later on when we get to chords. For the moment, I'll set it aside and answer a question of which you should have thought: If any key signature can stand for both a major and a minor key, how can you tell what the tonality of a piece is?

The answer is that you can't—not by the key signature alone. One way to tell is to listen: by the time you are finished with this book you should be able to hear the difference between major and minor. An easier way, though, is to look at the last note in the melody. Music doesn't always end on the tonic, but it usually does, and the last note of a piece is a good clue to its tonality.

I have been speaking about tonality as if it were fixed and immutable for each piece of music, but this is not so. Short pieces, like the simpler pop songs, the blues, and children's songs, usually stay in the same tonality throughout. Most other kinds of music change keys from time to time, sometimes as often as every few bars. Usually, though, no matter how many shifts of tonality a composer makes, he brings his music back to the original key at the end, in order to give a piece a sense of completeness, of having finished its journey. (A change of key, incidentally, is called a modulation.)

I have discussed the concept of tonality at some length here because of its importance to Western music, but the best way for you to really grasp it is through listening. When you hear a piece of music, try to find the tonic as the music goes along. Sing it; and then check to see if your note is the home note on which the music comes out at the end. With a little practice you will find that you can spot tonalities quite easily.

Intervals

At this point, let's take a little breather. We have come a fairly good distance. Starting with an infinite world of sounds, we have divided it into octaves, found sets of notes which we could group together in scales, related the notes in these scales to tonic notes, and even found a way to make little sets of scales. Our next step is to find ways to relate the notes within a given scale.

Our tool is something called intervals. An interval is simply the distance from one note to another. There are eighty-eight keys on a piano: the top note is an interval of eighty-seven half steps from the bottom. There are thirteen notes in a chromatic octave: the tope note is an interval of twelve half-steps from the bottom one.

This sounds simple enough and, in fact, it is. However, man in his usual fashion has found a way to make the study of intervals seem complicated.

The trouble is names. We call names—the naming of things— nomenclature. And there is no question but that nomenclature is the biggest stumbling block in music theory. When names are confusing, quite simple things become hard to grasp, and to put it bluntly, the names in music are a mess. The trouble is that they grew up slowly along with music theory. What would happen is that a theory or system of composing would die out, but the names it used would live on, getting attached to new systems which they didn't quite fit. The result is that today in music there are sometimes two different sets of names for things; in other cases there are no very good names; and in still others, a single name has two different meanings.

Someday, hopefully, somebody will reform musical nomenclature, but for the moment you are simply going to have to do some struggling with names. For my part, I will try to make myself as clear as possible; but if you find yourself having difficulty understanding something, you might check and make sure you've got the names right.

Now, names are going to confuse our study of intervals. To begin with, there are four different ways of naming the notes in any scale. One system of nomenclature you already know: do, re, mi, fa, sol, la, ti, do. The second system you also know, and goes according to the letters of the alphabet: A, B, C, D, E, F, G, A, combined with sharps and flats as necessary. There is a third system which gives each note in a scale a whole name. Starting with the tonic they are:

Tonic Supertonic Mediant Subdominant Dominant Submediant Leading Tone Tonic

Eventually you will want to know all these names but don't bother to memorize them now. You have more important things to worry about, among them the fourth system of nomenclature for the scales. In this system, each note is numbered, starting with the tonic. We always use Roman numerals:

As you see, when you get to the tonic note at the top of the scale, you don't number VIII, but I. However, just to confuse matters, we quite often want to go on numbering further, into the next octave, and when we do this, we don't start over again, but go on counting:

This numbering system is certainly a useful one and I will stick to it as much as possible. You should know, however, that "I" is almost invariably called simply that "tonic."

Now, the smallest interval you can make in Western music is a half step. The next smallest is two half-steps, the next three half-steps, and so forth, up to an interval made up of the highest and lowest notes people can ordinarily hear—about a hundred half-steps or so.

As I said, this all ought to be simple enough, but because of the nomenclature used for intervals, it isn't. The trouble is that musicians first began theorizing about intervals before the chromatic scale was in much use. The notes with which they were mainly concerned were the notes used in the diatonic scale. They named their intervals from the scale notes. Thus, the distance between the first note on a scale and the second was called an interval of a 2nd, or just a 2nd; the distance between the first and the third notes was a 3rd; between the first and sixth notes a 6th; and so forth, like this:

| Unison | 2nd | 3rd | 4th | 5th | 6th | 7th | octave | 9th | 10th etc. |

I've shown the notes in the example above as harmonies, as if they were to be played together, but the names apply just as well if the two notes of an interval are played one after the other.

In the example above we put only eight intervals inside the octave, counting the unison. There should be twelve. What happened to the interval of one half-step? Or of three half-steps? Or six? Or the rest of them?

The early musicians who began developing this theory didn't think of these other intervals as "real." They saw them only as variations of the eight main intervals. And they worked out these rules:

(1) Intervals of a 2nd, 3rd, 6th, and 7th are called major.

(2) Intervals of a 4th, a 5th, a unison, and an octave are called perfect.

(3) If you *add* a half step to any interval, you call it an augmented interval: an augmented 5th, an augmented 6th, etc.

(4) If you *subtract* a half step from a *major* interval, you call it minor: a minor 3rd, a minor 7th, etc.

(5) If you *subtract* a half step from a *perfect* interval, or a minor interval, you call it diminished: a diminished 4th, a diminished 5th, etc.

This nomenclature suited the musicians who worked it out, but it doesn't suit us very well. As you can see immediately, a lot of intervals end up having two names. The interval of six half-steps can be either a diminished 5th or an augmented 4th, for example.

(Which one we choose depends on complications we won't get into.) But worse, it tends to give the idea that, say, the interval of ten half-steps—the minor 7th—is only a version of the interval of eleven half-steps—the major 7th. Actually, if you listen to them, you can clearly hear them as having quite distinctly different qualities. It is a little as if we started thinking of green as merely a version of either yellow or blue, because it happens to come between them in the visible spectrum, the "scale," of colors.

But there is no help for it, and it is important that you grasp these names firmly, because everything we learn from now on depends on understanding intervals and their names. Here is the complete list.

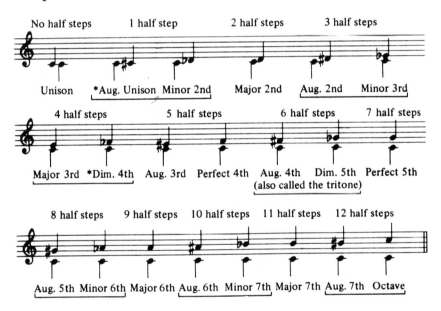

All of the examples of intervals I have given here are built on C. That is merely a matter of convenience, and you should not think that intervals have to be built from the first note of a scale. An interval is an interval regardless of whether it fits into a scale or not. For example, there is an interval of a perfect 4th between the 3rd and 6th of a major scale. Or to put it another way, between A above middle C and the D above that there will always be five half-steps, and the interval will always be a perfect 4th, regardless of keys or anything else. But this is not to say that any A and any D will always be a 5th apart. For one thing, if you move the D an octave higher you will have the interval of a 13th. But suppose you *drop* the D an octave, so that it is *beneath* the A. There are now seven half-steps between the two, and the interval becomes a perfect 5th.

So here is a way intervals can be related. A 4th upside down becomes a 5th. By the same token, a 3rd upside down becomes a 6th, and a 2nd upside down becomes a 7th. These inversions of intervals don't come out perfectly. A major 3rd becomes a minor 6th, a major 2nd becomes a minor 7th, and vice versa. The interesting thing about them, though, is that each pair of intervals tends to have something of the same sort of sound. Fourths and 5ths are sound sturdy, dry, and a little hollow. Thirds and 6ths are warmer, richer, perhaps a little sweet in sound. Seconds and 7ths are harsh, a little crackling.

And this brings us to what, after all, is the key to everything. Music is not words on paper, or black scratches on the staff: it is sounds in the ear. Knowing the distinctions in sound between one interval and the next is vitally important. You should play them over and over until you can recognize all intervals just by hearing them. This is not as difficult as it sounds. The best way to work is with a friend, taking turns playing intervals for the other person to guess. You will be amazed at how much you can learn in a couple of afternoons of concentrated listening.

3

Triads

IF YOU HAVE been listening to intervals, as I suggested you do in the last chapter, you will already have discovered that some of them seem "more harmonious," to use a vague term, than others. Throughout the long history of music, musicians have spent an enormous amount of time and effort working on exactly that problem: which intervals are acceptable to the ear, and which are not. It is worth taking a moment to see what they concluded.

In the days of classical antiquity music tended to be simple melody. Later on, it was decided that you could sound notes an octave apart together. For a considerable period all music was that simple.

Then, approximately eleven hundred years ago, musicians began duplicating their melodies a 4th or a 5th away. This simple step immediately opened up a great many new harmonic possibilities. Music became richer and more varied. This music, which built harmonies out of 4ths, 5ths, octaves, and unisons remained in fashion for several hundred years. Much of the music of the Catholic Church was composed during this period; you can still hear this old music sung in churches today. The best-known music of this type is called Gregorian chant, after Pope Gregory, who contributed to its development. To get an idea of how it sounds, here is a bit of a Gregorian chant, composed in the eleventh century:

But the harmonic possibilities of 4ths and 5ths, although vastly richer than those offered by simple octaves and unisons, were nonetheless limited. Composers began to try out other intervals, especially the 3rds. Gradually these queer new harmonies came to be accepted; and by the 1600's the interval of the 3rd was firmly established as the basic unit of harmony. It remains so to-day. The harmonies of virtually all the jazz, rock, pop, and most of the classical music you hear are organized around 3rds.

With the acceptance of 3rds as harmonious intervals, the 4th and 5th did not suddenly become disharmonious. As a matter of fact, taken by themselves are still considered the most "stable" of intervals—the intervals which seem to the ear most harmonious. Here, then, is our scale of values:

(1) 3rds, 4ths, 5ths, and octaves are considered *consonant* intervals. The word *consonance* comes from Latin words meaning "sounding with." Consonant intervals are made up of two notes which go together well. They seem to fit together.

(2) 2nds and 7ths are considered *dissonant* intervals. They

are made up of notes which seem to sound against each other—which don't fit exactly right.

Dissonance, however, is not discord. Discord is a word we use to describe sounds which are distinctly unpleasant, verging on noise. Hitting a bunch of black and white keys on the piano together with your elbow will produce a discord. In fact, any two adjacent keys played together (a minor 2nd) is discordant if played by itself.

Dissonance is a useful part of music. I will have more to say about this when I talk about melody. For the moment just let me say that one consonant sound after another begins to seem too sweet after awhile. Music needs dissonance to give it variety and strength.

I make this point, because as we get into chords we will find that some are dissonant. But before we begin our discussion of chords I want to make the point that in music we quite often find that there is more than one way of looking at a thing. That is, you can explain it in two or more different ways. Sometimes both explanations are equally good. Sometimes one is more helpful than another in certain situations. In other cases neither way of seeing a thing explains it correctly: you have to look at it from two different points of view to understand how it works.

This last is the case with chords. There are two basic ways of looking at them, and you really need both of these explanations to understand what they are and how they work. You can think of chords as being taken from scales or as being built up out of intervals. I'll begin with the scale explanation.

From this point of view, then, a chord is made by taking *every other* note from a diatonic scale. You can go on doing this as far up the scale as you want, but you must have at least three notes to make a chord, otherwise you have merely an interval.

The above is a C-major scale. By taking the first, third, and fifth notes from it, and stacking them up, you will get a C-major chord. A three-note chord like this is called a *triad* (pronounced *try'-add*), a word which comes from the Latin for "three."

In the same way, from a minor scale you can derive a minor triad:

In this example we have derived a G-minor chord from a G-minor scale. It should be obvious, then, that chords and scales have some things in common: their tonality and their modality (whether they are in the major *mode* or minor *mode*, or some other mode). We cannot say that chords and scales are the same thing; obviously they are not. But we can say that a C-major chord suggests to the ear a C-major scale; and the other way around, a C-major scale suggests a C-major chord. A minor scale suggests a certain minor chord, and a minor chord suggests the same minor scale. You can see, thus, that chords and scales are very much part and parcel of the same thing, spinning around each other like the earth and the moon.

But triads are not the end of it. I said earlier that you can go on taking every other note from a diatonic scale for as long as you want to, like this:

In this example we have taken eight notes from a scale and piled them up to make one huge chord. If you examine it for a moment, you will notice two interesting things about it. One is that the last note is a C—the same note as the first note, or tonic, only two octaves higher. At this point the series begins to repeat itself. So, for all practical purposes, this huge chord is really limited to the first seven notes.

The second interesting thing that you might notice is that the fifth note in our great chord is a D, which is the same as the second note in the scale, only an octave higher. The sixth note is an F, which is the same as the fourth note in the scale, only an octave higher. And the seventh note, similarly, is an octave above the sixth note in a scale. The notes in this great C chord then are:

C, E, G, B, D, F, A

They are the seven notes of the original scale. If you bring the top three notes of a huge chord like this down an octave, you will have put the scale back together again:

And now we have to get back into nomenclature problems again. Each note in this great chord has a name. Its name is the interval it makes with the tonic, like this:

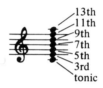

This is easy enough to learn; it is merely counting by odd numbers. You absolutely should get these names for the parts of the chords down pat, otherwise you won't be able to make any sense out of the rest of my discussion of chords—or the rest of the book, for that matter. And don't get confused: we use the terms 3rd, 5th, 7th, and so forth for intervals, and we use them also for the notes in a chord. This is not quite as silly as it seems; when you talk about the 3rd of a chord, what you are really saying is "the note an interval of a 3rd from the tonic," so that these two uses of this set of terms come down almost to the same thing. But get it right: a 5th is an interval; it's also a certain note in a chord.

In all of the examples which I have given you so far, concerning the making of chords from scales, I have begun with the tonic.

But you don't have to begin with the tonic. You can begin with II, the second note of the scale:

or with III:

In fact, you can begin making chords from any note in the scale. And this now is going to lead us into some problems. If, out of a C-major scale, you take a chord beginning with D, is the tonic of the chord C or D? Is it still a major chord? What happens when you go on further up the scale?

Here's another problem. We made our D chord from a C-*major* scale, but we can also make it from a *D-minor* scale.

As a matter of fact, you can derive that same chord from a number of scales. You can get it by beginning on the third note of a B♭-major scale; the fourth note of an A-minor scale; the fifth note of a G-minor scale; and the sixth note of an F-major scale.

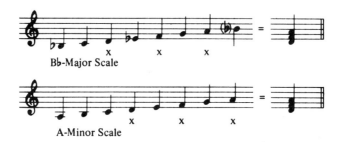

We clearly have some problems. A chord can't be both major and minor, and it can't have a half-dozen tonics. Our scale explanation for chords is at this point becoming useless to us. We have learned that we can make chords from scales; but we obviously are going to have to learn some other things about them, too.

If you take another look at some of the chords I used in the foregoing examples, you will notice that each note in them is either three or four half-steps away from the ones on either side of it—that is, the notes are either a major 3rd or a minor 3rd apart. This tells us something: that chords are made up of 3rds. And so we now go to another way of looking at chords. The rule is this. A chord can be made by piling up 3rds:

They can be either major or minor 3rds, and we can put the majors and minors in any arrangement we choose:

Minor	Minor	Minor	Minor	Minor	
Major	Minor	Major	Major	Minor	
	Major	Major	Minor	Minor	
		Minor	Major	Minor	etc.
			Major	Minor	

This is going to prove a very useful way of looking at chords, because it will allow us to make some chords which you simply can't
derive from *any* scale. It will also help us to solve those problems
of tonality and modality.

The tonality problem is easy to solve. The tonic of any chord
built from thirds is its bottom note, forever and always. (Later on
I will show you ways to turn chords upside down, so that the
tonic comes out in other places, but so long as the chord is in
what we call root position—that is, one third on top of the next
—the bottom note is the tonic.)

The problem of modality—whether a chord is major or minor
or something else—is not quite as easy to solve, but it is not very
difficult, either. To understand how it works, we will forget
about great chords and concentrate on triads.

A triad has three notes and is therefore made up of two 3rds,
one on top of the other:

There are only four possible combinations of major and minor
3rds that can be used to make up a triad. Here they are, with the
names they have been given:

major triad	*minor triad*	*diminished triad*	*augmented triad*
minor 3rd	major 3rd	minor 3rd	major 3rd
over	over	over	over
major 3rd	minor 3rd	minor 3rd	major 3rd

The major and minor triads can be derived from major and minor
scales, if you begin with the tonic. The diminished and aug-

mented don't relate nearly so neatly from scales. The diminished chord can be derived by starting on the seventh note of a major scale, and the augmented chord can be derived by starting on a certain note in one version of a minor scale. But it is easier to think of them simply as piles of 3rds.

Now let's see how they look in musical notation:

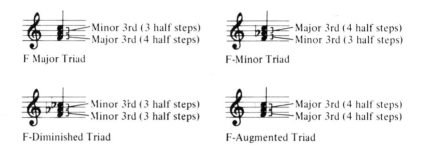

The sharps and flats in the example above should give you a good idea of how you change one of these four chords to the next. A major triad has four half-steps in the bottom 3rd, and three half-steps in the top 3rd. A minor triad has the 3rds reversed. Thus, simply by lowering the middle note a half step you change a major triad into a minor. Augmented and diminished chords are produced out of the others in similar fashion. It is quite easy, then, to shift from one of this set of triads to the other. Let's look at another set, to make sure you have the idea:

Ab-Major   Ab-Minor   Ab-Diminished   Ab-Augmented
  Triad   Triad   Triad   Triad

Notice the Ebb (E double-flat) in the Ab diminished-chord above. An Ebb is the same as a D; why not simply write an Ab-diminished chord this way?

The answer is that the interval between Cb and D is not a minor 3rd, but an augmented 2nd. To be sure, the ear can't tell the difference, but the rule is that chords must be made up of 3rds, not 2nds. Since we can write the chord either way, we ought to use the one that sticks closest to our logic, in order not to confuse ourselves any more than necessary. You will occasionally see double-flats and double-sharps in music; this is why. (The sign for a double-sharp, incidentally, is *not* ♯ ♯, but ✖.)

Major, minor, diminished, and augmented: these four types of triads are the basic stock of nearly all of our music, no matter what kind. You can, of course, build all four of them on each of the twelve tones in the chromatic scale, giving you forty-eight different triads all told. These forty-eight basic chords can be combined in an astounding number of ways. The richness and diversity they offer musicians has been exploited millions of times, and the possibilities still have not been exhausted. Fresh music based on these forty-eight triads is written every day.

Because these four types of triads are so vital to any music you listen to or attempt to create, you should learn them absolutely cold. You should memorize which notes go into each of the forty-eight chords. This sounds like a lot of work, but it isn't. Begin by figuring out the twelve major chords and learning them. Once you know the majors, the rest of them are simple. All you have to know is how to change a major into a minor, diminished, or augmented chord.

But most important, I must remind you once again that music is not notes on paper, it is sounds in the ear. You should play these four chords over and over until the distinct individual sounds of major, minor, diminished, and augmented are stuck in your ear. Get a friend to work with you, the way I suggested you do with the intervals. Learning to hear the triads is a lot easier than learning to hear the intervals: there are only four types, after all. I assure you, the effort will pay off every time you sit down to play, write music, or simply listen.

4

Seventh Chords

IN THE BEGINNING of the last chapter we saw how to make a great chord of seven notes, by taking every other note from two successive scales, like this:

We confined ourselves then to talking about triads—chords made up of the three bottom notes of this large chord. But you can just as easily take the bottom four notes with which to work or the bottom five, and so forth. In this chapter we are going to deal with chords using the bottom four notes. They are called 7th chords because their top note is a 7th away from the tonic.

In the last chapter we made four types of triads—major, minor, augmented, and diminished—by piling up combinations of major and minor 3rds. But there is another way to change one to another: by raising or lowering one or two of the notes a half step.

And now this brings us to a rule: *in any major chord, you can always raise or lower by a half step any of the notes except the tonic.* (This practice is sometimes known as "altering" the chord, but the term "altered chords" is used in different ways by different music theorists, and I would just as soon stay away from it here.)

Theoretically, in any case, you can raise or lower any note in a chord a half step, but in actual practice you can't. For example, if you augment—that is raise—the 3rd, you get the 4th. E is the 3rd in a C chord; raise it a half step and it becomes E♯, which is the same as F—the 4th. Similarly if you augment the 7th you get the tonic; if you diminish the 11th you get a 3rd, and so forth. Furthermore, if you go through the great chord raising and lowering its notes indiscriminantly, you can get some very odd sounds:

The above chord is possible in theory, but if you play it on the piano you will find it extremely dissonant—not to say discordant. It can be used, of course, but music filled with chords like this would be extremely jangling to the nerves. My point is that although in theory you can develop a number of variations on any chord, many of them are not used often, if at all, in practice.

As a general thing, our other method of making chords—by piling up 3rds—keeps us out of real troubles. Any combination of major and minor 3rds piled on top of each other is bound to sound reasonably harmonious. To be sure, this method gives us somewhat fewer variations of each chord, and you obviously ought to know how to make some of the extreme chords by diminishing and augmenting various notes in it. But as a beginning you are better off working with a few important chords and saving the less common chords for future study.

This is why. You can in theory make eighteen different 7th chords by diminishing and augmenting the notes in them. Some of these chords are so extreme that they can't really be played: the ear insists upon hearing them as something else. By the stacking-up-of-3rds method, you can make eight 7th chords, most of them the same as ones made by the first method.

Out of this pile of 7th chords I am going to talk about only four. They are, however, the 7th chords which you hear most of the time and they will be far more useful to you than all the other possibilities put together.

Let us begin with what is called a major-7th chord. It is made by adding a major 3rd to a major triad like this.

You can also think of it simply as the four bottom notes of our great chord, without any augmenting or diminishing. As you will notice, in the above F-major-7th chord, the top note is an E, only a half step from the tonic. The ear has a very strong wish for this note to move on up to the F, and this effect gives the major-7th chord a bittersweet, haunting feeling. This haunting, somewhat sad feeling is useful to composers of popular songs; they are likely to use them often in songs of parting, sorrow, and unhappy love.

At this point we are back to the problem of nomenclature again. One of the problems with musical abbreviations is that the words major and minor both begin with "m." A little thing like this can cause a tremendous amount of confusion unless we are quite careful to get it all straight. Thus we have this rule: Capital "M" stands for major, small "m" stands for minor. Actually, it would be simpler if everybody used the symbols "maj." and "min.," but they don't. In any case there sometimes isn't enough room on the music.

The symbol for a major-7th chord, thus, is M7, like this: CM7, E♭M7, and so forth. The symbol for a minor-7th chord, the next one we are going to take up, is therefore m7.

The minor-7th chord is made up of a minor triad with a minor 3rd added. That is, both the 3rd and the 7th of the chord are lowered by a half step:

This chord is a quite common one. There are plenty of examples of it in the classical composers, and it is especially widely used in all forms of modern popular music, most particularly jazz. Rock-and-roll players, however, have made a special pet of this chord. You can hear it over and over in almost any sort of rock—so much so that the sound of the minor-7th chord has become one of the special characteristics of that music.

The third of the four most important of the 7th chords is what we call the diminished 7th. It is made of a minor 3rd added to a diminished triad. It looks like this:

As you can see, the 7th has to be lowered two half-steps to bring it a minor 3rd away from the 5th. The note a full step below the 7th of course is the 6th, so in actual practice the diminished-7th chord is often written like this, despite the rule about 3rds.

The diminished-7th chord is quite an interesting one. In its way, it is a specialty of itself. It is made up of three minor-3rds stacked one on top of the other, and if you add one more minor-3rd, making a stack of four minor-3rds, you will come out on a note an octave above the bottom note. And if you go on adding more minor-3rds you will simply repeat the chord again.

In theory, of course, the bottom note of the diminished 7th, like the bottom note of any chord, is the tonic. In actual practice, however, the diminished 7th doesn't really seem to have a tonic. It lacks tonality. If you play its notes one after another like a melody, you get the feeling that it never quite ends, never quite settles down, but would just as soon go on and on:

Because the chord spread out thus into a melody seems endless, it gives a feeling of suspense. Composers have taken great advantage of this fact to create effects of mystery and suspense, especially in background music to movies and television shows.

A second interesting fact about the diminished-7th chord is that because it doesn't have a real tonic, you can play it with any of its notes on the bottom and get the same effect:

Although the above chords each have a different bottom note, they really sound very nearly the same, and composers use them as if they were. And this then brings us to one more fact about diminished-7th chords: there are only three of them. If you think about it a minute you can see why. Make diminished-7th chords on a sequence of notes from the chromatic scale, like this:

D♯ and E♭ are the same note, of course. The diminished-7th chord on D♯ is thus the same as the one on C, except that it has a different one of its notes on the bottom. The diminished-7th chord with G♭ on the bottom will also be the same, and so will the one with A on the bottom. All of these four diminished 7ths, thus, are merely versions of each other. And the same thing applies to the other diminished-7th chords: each one has three nearly-identical twins. So in the end, you really have only three diminished-7ths chords, each coming in four almost identical versions.

Besides creating effects of suspense, diminished-7th chords have another useful function. Because they never seem to quite belong anywhere, it is easy to use them as a steppingstone between two keys. Lazy piano players put them in all the time when they want to modulate from one key to another without much trouble. The symbol for the diminished-7th chord is simply dim7.

I have saved for last the most important of all the 7th chords —the so-called dominant 7th. It is more important than any other chord in music except the major and minor triads. In fact, it is probably even more important than the minor triad.

The dominant 7th is made up of a minor 3rd added to a major triad:

It gets its name from the fifth note of the scale, which is called the dominant. If you build a chord from a major scale beginning on the 5th, you will get a dominant-7th chord, like this:

Here, out of a Bb-major scale we have made an F dominant-7th chord. It is important to remember this fact, because when we get into our study of chord relationships, we will find that a B♭-major chord and the F dominant 7th made from the B♭ scale have a special relationship. Or, to put it another way, the dominant 7th built on the 5th of a major or minor triad has an extremely close relationship to that triad. Here are some examples of triads and their dominant 7ths.

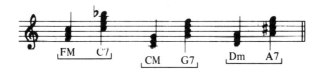

This relationship between a chord and its dominant 7th is the strongest in music. I will get into this more deeply in a later chapter, but let me say now that music of all kinds—classical, pop, rock, jazz, blues, folk—is simply jam-packed with dominant-7th chords, usually moving to their tonics. Vast, complex theories have been worked out to show that Western music is based entirely on this dominant–tonic relationship. As a matter of fact, the blues are nothing more than a repeated expression of this basic relationship, which helps to explain why they have so captured the imagination of musicians. If you learn nothing else out of this book you must absolutely get a death-grip on the dominant–tonic relationship. As a matter of fact, with that tool alone you can understand half the music you come up against. Just to give you a feeling for this relationship, play the two chords below:

That particular chord movement of the dominant 7th to its related major chord is undoubtedly utterly familiar to you; you have heard it thousands of times. You notice in the above example that I have used as a symbol for dominant-7th chords just a 7.

Let's now look over our four 7th chords once more for review:

There still remain for your investigation other 7th chords, which you can make by adding major and minor 3rds to triads or by diminishing or augmenting notes in the 7th chord. You will certainly want to experiment with these other 7th chords as time goes along. However, I strongly advise you to concentrate on the four 7th-chords we have been talking about for the present. Like intervals and triads, each has its distinctive sound. If you work on listening to them, as you did with the triads—or at least should have done with the triads—you will learn quickly to identify them with your ear. I cannot repeat too often that music is not black specks on paper: it is sounds in the ear.

5

Ninth, Eleventh, and Thirteenth Chords

THE FOUR TRIADS and the four most important 7th chords make up a good portion of the music you usually hear. Since you can build all eight of these chords on any of the twelve notes in the chromatic scale you have ninety-six, all told—or really eighty-seven, counting off for so many of the diminished 7ths being the same. This group of chords contains a vast richness of possibilities, enough to last a composer a lifetime. In point of fact, the whole great body of work of such composers as Bach, Handel, and Scarlatti is based largely on these chords.

Yet we can go further. We can add one more 3rd to make 9th chords; and another for 11ths; and yet another for 13ths. Over the past hundred years or so these chords have come to be used more and more frequently. This is especially true in jazz where today 9ths are almost as common as 7ths—so common, indeed, that a simple triad is now rarely heard. We must explore some of these more-advanced chords.

The exploration, however, is fairly heavy going. We can make these 9th, 11th, and 13th chords by stacking up major or minor 3rds on top of 7ths in a wide variety of ways. And if we start adding up all the possible combinations of triads, 7th, 9th, 11th, and 13th chords, we find that we can make well over a hundred different chords on any tonic.

The very idea is enough to exhaust anyone. Fortunately most of these hundred chords are possible only in theory. In practice many of them turn out to be identical to some other chord; others are terribly discordant; and still others confuse the ear as to their tonalities, so that you're never sure what they're meant to be. Nonetheless, musicians, especially jazz musicians, have fifteen 9th chords which they occasionally use, as well as eight or ten different 11th chords, and perhaps four or five 13th chords.

Using these chords so that they sound well is a complex business. Only when you have gotten quite far in your studies of composition will you need to worry about all these advanced chords. However, there are a few of them that you can profitably learn to understand.

The first of these is the ordinary 9th-chord—just a minor 3rd stuck on top of a major-7th chord, like this:

The ordinary 9th-chord, then, is quite simple to construct. However, just as you can lower a 3rd, 5th, or 7th by a half step to get a different chord, so you can lower the 9th a half step as well. A 9th of this kind is called a diminished 9th.

But you can't safely make a diminished 9th out of any 7th-chord. In a C chord, for example, the major 7th is a B and the diminished 9th is a D♭. The two notes are only a whole step apart—too close for comfort in a chord which is already fairly dissonant. The best rule, therefore, is to make *diminished 9ths* only out of *dominant-7th* chords. Here, then, are two useful new chords, the 9th, and the diminished 9th:

FM9   F7♭9

As I have suggested, there are a great many other varieties of 9th chords. They are much less frequently used than the two I have given you, and in any case they present too many problems for the beginner to struggle with.

In a way, 11th chords present fewer problems than 9ths. The 11th is the same as the 4th, an octave higher. If you lower an 11th a half step you will get a 3rd an octave higher. Practically speaking, therefore, there is no such thing as a diminished 11th. You can augment an 11th by raising it a half step; but, as with many types of 9ths, these augmented 11ths are too tricky for the beginning student to deal with.

Because the 11th is only a half step away from the 3rd (really a half step plus an octave, of course) it doesn't work well in major chords. The best rule, therefore, is to add 11ths only to chords with minor 3rds in them. And, since the 11th chord has quite a bit of dissonance in it, it is a good idea not to add the 11th to diminished-9th chords. In other words, 11ths should be added only to chords with minor 3rds and major 9ths. Here are the two most important ones:

As far as 13th chords are concerned, the less you have to do with them at this stage the better. However, there is one type of 13th chord you ought to know about. The 13th note of the scale is the same as the 6th. And the 6th is an extremely popular note in music, especially in jazz and some types of pop songs. It is so popular, in fact, that arrangers, composers, and jazz improvisers simply add it to triads without trying to justify it as a 13th or anything else. During the big swing-band period of the 1930's and 1940's the 6th was added to chords wholesale, so that you hardly ever heard a plain, ordinary major triad. (Today it is the 9th that arrangers use far too often.)

The point is, in any case, that legitimately the 6th ought to be called a 13th; after all, a chord is supposed to be made up of 3rds, and the 6th is not a 3rd away from anything in a chord. Practically speaking, however, musicians simply call it a 6th, and they add it to major and minor triads.

You can't however, add a 6th (or 13th—whichever you chose to call it) into any chord. It makes too close an interval to be used with 7ths, and it doesn't sound well with diminished 9ths. The best rule is to add 6ths only to major and minor triads, and to 9th chords in place of the 7th. Below are the four most useful possibilities:

FM6   Fm6   FM6+9   Fm6+9

The handful of advanced chords that I have given you are plenty to start with, but there are, as I have said, many others. The rules that I have laid down are not hard and fast. You can use a diminished 9th, or a 6th, with a major 7th if you want that harsh, abrasive sound. There's no law against it, and composers have done it. And you will of course want to experiment with these other, more tricky, varieties of advanced chords, just to find out what they sound like. But the handful I have given you will prove the most useful.

Chord Symbols

As you probably have gathered by now, we are running into problems of nomenclature again. As a matter of fact chord symbols are one of the worst nomenclature-messes we have in music. This again is because the symbols were invented piecemeal; nobody ever sat down and worked out a complete system. As a result we have in some cases two or more symbols for one thing and none for another. Worse, different arrangers use different sets of symbols so that sometimes even experienced players get confused.

Unfortunately, you are going to have to struggle with this confusion of terms. In music today it is not enough simply to be able to read notes: you have to be able to read chord symbols as well. What has happened is that today a great deal of music is either not written down, or only written down in chord symbols. This is especially true of rock players, many of whom can't read notes at all. Although most jazz players today are good readers, they are also constantly called upon to deal with chord symbols. Indeed, most of the small groups that play for dances, weddings, and parties don't read music, either. Musicians today are expected to be able to improvise melodies, harmonies, and accompaniments just from knowing what the chords of a piece of music are.

Later on in this book I will show you some things about working out harmonies from chords. For the moment, let's just see if we can't straighten out the symbols.

In music today you will often see two types of chord notations. One is a simple chord-progression chart. Here is a sample of a chord chart for a simple blues-progression:

‖ B♭7 / / / | E♭7 / / / | B♭7 / / / | B♭7 / / / | E♭7 / / / | E♭m / / / |

| B♭7 / / / | G7 / / / | Cm7 / / / | F7 / / / | B♭ / / / | B♭ / / / ‖

In the example above, the bigger lines are measure lines, and the little lines indicate that the chord is to be repeated for three more beats. A somewhat clearer way of notating chords to indicate how many beats each chord gets is this:

‖ B♭7 E♭7
   / / / / | = ‖ B♭7 / E♭7 / |

But perhaps even more common than chord-progression charts are what are called "lead sheets." A lead sheet contains the melody, the chord symbols, and the lyrics, if any, of a piece of music. Except in big swing-bands, and of course in classical music, where everybody's part is written out, musicians today work almost exclusively from lead sheets. Even if they don't actually have the lead sheet in front of them, they have it in their heads: rock, jazz, and especially pop musicians have memorized the chords and melodies to hundreds, sometimes thousands, of songs. (Don't be discouraged: they learned them one at a time over a period of years, mainly by playing them.) Here is a section of a typical lead sheet:

It should now be clear to you that beginning to be able to understand chord symbols is vitally important in modern music. So let's then review the ones we've learned:

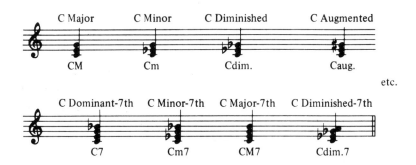

This notation covers a number of basic chords, but it doesn't help with the 9ths, 11ths, and 13ths, as well as some other 7th chords. For example, so far we have no symbol for a 7th added to an augmented triad. At this point, however, you have too many things to worry about already, without struggling with the symbols for the more complex chords. However, I have put a chart of the complete system in the back of the book (see Appendix E) so that you can familiarize yourself with it when you feel ready for it.

6

Inverting, Doubling, and Omitting

Inversions

UNTIL NOW, for the sake of clarity, I have been talking about chords as if they always sat with their tonics on the bottom and climbed upwards in stacks of 3rds. But as any of you know who have studied the piano or guitar, chords don't always come in this straightforward manner. For one thing, they can be turned upside down. For another, you can sometimes leave parts of them out. And for a third thing, you can sometimes add notes an octave away from the ones you already have.

You can perform any of these operations on a chord without changing its essential nature. You can do all these things at once, if you want. As a matter of fact, composers do these things so often to chords that in many pieces of music you won't find one chord in its plain, original form. Now, let's take up these three ways of treating a chord one at a time.

Turning a chord upside down is called "inverting" it. Actually, it is not a matter of turning it upside down as much as it is of having some note other than the tonic on the bottom. The way you do this is to swing the tonic and perhaps some other of the notes up an octave so they are now on top, like this:

You are perfectly free to arrange a chord with any of its notes on the bottom. As a matter of fact, you can set it up with its notes in any order you want. You are free to do this not because I say so, or because the great masters of music say so: you can do it because the ear says so. No matter which way you arrange your chord, the ear will still hear it as basically the same thing. If it's a G chord it will still hear the G as the tonic, even if the G is on top. It will still hear it as major, minor, diminished, or augmented; or as a 7th, 9th, or whatever.

Now I am not saying, of course, that an inverted chord will sound exactly as it did originally. If you spread a D-major chord across the keyboard with, say, the A way down at the bottom, the D in the middle, and the F♯ way up near the top, you are going to hear a quite different sound than if you play the notes together in the middle of the piano with the D on the bottom. Nonetheless, I repeat: the basic nature of the chord will remain the same.

A chord with its tonic on the bottom and the other notes going up in thirds is in *root* position. A chord with the 3rd on the bottom is in the first inversion; a chord with the 5th on the bottom is in the second inversion:

root
position

first
inversion

second
inversion

Similarly, a 7th chord with the 7th on the bottom is in the third inversion; a 9th chord with the 9th on the bottom is in the fourth inversion; and so on.

Where the other notes fall doesn't matter. A chord with the 3rd on the bottom is in the first inversion, regardless of whether the tonic or the 5th is on top:

root
position

first inversion

Nor does it matter whether the chords are major, minor, or whatever: the names still apply. And it should be clear too that it doesn't matter how many octaves apart the notes are. The inversion remains the same, no matter how spread out the notes are. What matters is which note is on the bottom.

Now let me repeat: although inversions don't change a chord's essential nature, they don't leave it sounding exactly the same either. The subtle difference between one inversion and the next is something you will take up in more advanced study of theory. However, I will say this: second inversions, with the 5th of the chord on the bottom, seem to be less final, less solid, than chords in root position or first inversion. The reason is that chords in second inversion have an interval of a 4th on the bottom, which the ear finds a little unsettled.

Doubling

Inverting a chord, thus, is one stunt you can do to it. The second is to add more of the same notes an octave or more away. For example, a D-minor triad is made up of D, F, A. You can add any number of any of these notes without changing the essential nature of the chord:

There are six notes in the chord above, but they are all D's, F's, and A's; the chord is still a D-minor triad. This practice is called doubling. You don't, however, have to double all the notes. You can double any of them; in fact you can triple one and leave the others alone:

The practice of doubling is exceedingly common. Pianists tend to double something in every triad, especially the tonics, and guitar players, who have six strings at their disposal, are likely to double one or two notes in a chord simply because it is easier to play all six strings at once than just three or four. The piano, bass, and guitar in a jazz rhythm-section double many notes, and of course a symphony orchestra doubles notes in a chord all up and down the full range of its instrumentation. Indeed, the most final, stable, satisfactory ending-chord of all is one in which the tonic is doubled:

Doubling does not simply mean having two instruments play the same note. This happens all the time in church choirs, school bands, and symphony orchestras where twenty violins may be playing the same part. The term *doubling* is used primarily when the notes are an octave or more apart.

As with inversions, doublings don't change the essential nature of a chord: you still have a B♭-minor chord no matter how many B♭'s you put in. But again, a chord full of doublings is not exactly the same as it is without them. Composers and music theorists have worked out quite elaborate sets of rules for the shades of difference between one doubling and another. These rules are something that can best be left to advanced theory. However, I will give you one important rule: if you have to double a note in a triad, it is better to pick the tonic or 5th rather than the 3rd.

Omitting

So much for doublings. The third trick you can perform on a chord is to leave notes out. On the surface, this seems to contradict everything I have said so far. And to some extent it does. After all, if a chord must have three notes, how can you leave one out?

Of course you can't, in theory. In actual practice, however, situations often come up when you *have* to omit one or more notes from a chord. Most of these problems have to do with voice-leading, which we will take up in a later chapter. The most obvious sort of thing, however, is when three voices—three trumpets in a symphony orchestra, or three saxophones in a dance band, say—are called upon to play a 7th chord. There are four notes in the chord, but only three instruments on which to play them. And the question then arises: Which note should be omitted?

Here again a good many rules have been worked out by composers and arrangers to deal with the omitting of notes. I will give you just a few of the basic ones:

(1) In most cases the ear misses the 5th less than the other notes in a chord.

(2) The 3rd should never be omitted from a triad. For one, the 3rd tells whether a chord is major or minor. For another, with the 3rd left out you have only harmony in 4ths and 5ths. The 3rd can sometimes be omitted from extended chords like 7ths and 9ths, but in general the 3rd should be omitted only with great caution.

(3) You obviously can't omit the characteristic note of any chord—the 7th in a 7th chord, the 9th in a 9th, and so forth.

(4) Surprisingly, it is quite permissible to omit the tonic. Sometimes it is the best choice. Suppose three saxophones are playing a 7th chord, and the melody happens to be on the 5th, a quite common occurence. You can't omit the 5th without changing the melody; you can't omit the 7th without changing the character of the chord. Your choice is between omitting the tonic or the 3rd; and you might decide that you change the quality of the chord least by leaving out the tonic—although it is permissible to omit the 3rd in a dominant-7th chord.

In thinking about omissions, you have to remember that chords don't usually stand alone. They are preceded and followed by others. Thus, if a tonality has been established, the ear will go on hearing it a bit even if the tonic disappears. Here is a good example of that effect:

The second chord in the example above could be called an E-diminished triad. However, the first chord has established a firm tonality, and since two of the notes remain the same in both chords, the ear will probably go on hearing the same tonality—so that the B♭ is heard as the minor 7th of a C chord, rather than the diminished 5th of an E chord.

Doubling, omission, and inversion, then, are three basic operations you can perform on any chord. They are all done constantly. As I said earlier, in music most chords have one or another done to them, and frequently two or even all three. It is not uncommon to see chords in which one note is omitted and another doubled—something which may seem silly in theory but which is often a good idea in practice.

And this again brings us back to the point that music is not theory, it is sounds in the ear. None of the rules on inversion, doubling, and omitting is hard and fast. They can all be broken when the ear says to break them. Professional musicians break them all the time. As a matter of fact, you quite often run into situations where you can't keep one rule without breaking another.

Nonetheless, the rules I have given here can be useful. As you experiment with them, you will find that they do help make music palatable to the ear.

7

Chord Relationships

WE HAVE SPENT a good portion of this book learning how to put chords together. However, if you have gotten a good grip on how chords are built, the time has been well spent. Once you get an understanding of chords you have come a long way out of the musical woods. At this point you should be able to see some daylight ahead.

Now, to recap just for a moment, we learned at the beginning that the basic building blocks of music are tones. We found next that you can organize tones into pairs to make intervals. And we then found that you can put intervals together to make chords. Quite obviously, we must now find ways to put chords together to make something else. And in this case something else is complete musical pieces.

But to do this we must change our thinking about chords slightly. Up to this point we have seen chords as a group of notes played together, all at once. Now you must realize that a chord can be stated—"expressed," "said"—just as well one note after another:

The two examples above are of course not the same. One is a D7 "chord." The other is a bit of melody. Yet the melody is made up of the notes from the D7 chord, and the ear will quite clearly get the whole sense of D7 regardless of the way it is played. But here's another way to put it:

This little bit of melody looks even less like a D7 chord than the first bit. The notes aren't even, they don't come in any special order, and some of them are repeated. Nonetheless, this small melody quite clearly says D7, as you can easily find out by listening to it.

There is a great deal more than this to be said on the subject of the relationship of chords to melody. I am going to take it up in detail in a later chapter. For the moment, however, I want you to realize that from now on when I talk about chords I mean the word in both ways—as melody, or as notes played all at once.

Chord Progressions

Virtually all Western music is based on sequences of chords. We usually call these sequences "chord progressions," or as musicians often put it, "chord changes," or just "changes." Even the simplest songs that children sing, like *Happy Birthday* and *Pop Goes the Weasel,* are based on chord progressions.

Furthermore, in most instances each piece of music, no matter how long or complicated, has only *one* chord progression. There are some exceptions to this, both in very modern music and in some of the older music, but for the most part the chords in a song come alone one at a time, like the freight cars in a railroad train.

Unlike freight cars, however, they are not all of the same length. Sometimes a chord is repeated over and over, or lingers on and on, for minutes at a time. At other times the chords change every measure, or even every beat. Indeed, some of the great jazz players will run through a chord every second when they are improvising. Still, on and on they go, one after another. Our problem now is to find out how to line chords up in an order that makes musical sense. And at this point we are once again faced with the old problem of nomenclature.

Chord Symbols

As you have learned, every chord has some sort of a name: E♭M, Fm, C7, and so forth. But in talking about chords, musicians are very likely to use another system of names which helps to make clear chord relations.

The way this system works is this. You may have forgotten, but early in this book I showed you a system of nomenclature for diatonic scales based on Roman numerals:

E-Major Scale

I   II   III   IV   V   VI   VII   I

In this system, as you can see, the tonic of a scale is called I, and the other notes are numbered on up the scale until you reach the tonic again. There is a similar system for chords. It depends on the fact that most pieces of music have a tonality.

For a piece of music in the key of C major, we number all C chords I. We number D chords II, E chords III, and so forth. It is a little as if we were making a scale of chords. Or, to put it another way, we are making a chord on each note in that scale, and giving that chord the same number as the scale note it is made on. In the key of C, the chords would be numbered like this:

$$\text{I} \quad \text{II} \quad \text{III} \quad \text{IV} \quad \text{V} \quad \text{VI} \quad \text{VII} \quad \text{I}$$

The trick, though, is to make sure you are working with the right scale. For example, in an F scale, the fourth note is not B, but B♭; a IV chord in F is therefore a B♭ chord, not a B chord. Similarly, in the key of F minor, the third note of the scale is not A, but A♭. Thus, in F minor, a III chord is an A♭ chord, not an A chord.

These numbers are used for any type of chord based on the same note on the scale. In the key of G, for example, the second note is A. In our Roman-numeral system of numbering, an A chord would be called II regardless of whether it is major, minor, 7th, or anything else. In order to make clear what *type* of chord is meant, we simply use our old symbols: IIm, IIaug, IIm7, and so forth.

Now, if you think about it for a moment, you will see that an A chord can have a variety of different names. In the key of G it is called a II chord, but in B♭ it is a VII chord, because A is the seventh note of a B♭ scale; and in the key of D it is a V chord, because it is the fifth note of a D scale.

This should be clear enough. But what about chords built on notes that don't belong to the scale? For example, in the key of

E♭, the fourth scale-note is A♭. A isn't in an E♭ scale at all. The answer is to put a sharp or flat in front of the Roman numeral to raise it or lower it properly. In the key of E♭, A♭ is the IV chord. An A chord is called a ♯ IV chord.

Offhand, this new system of numbering may seem like an unnecessary nuisance. It has, however, a real use. It allows musicians to talk about chord progressions and chord relationships in the abstract. That is to say, you can talk about types of relationships that are good for any key. You might say, for example, "When the song *I Got Rhythm* is played in B♭, the bridge begins on a D7 chord; and a similar relationship applies when the song is in other keys." It is a lot simpler and clearer to say, "The bridge of *I Got Rhythm* begins on the III7 chord," and leave it at that.

In any case, musicians use this Roman-numeral system of naming chords constantly. You will always hear them talking about I–V relationships, or the III–VI–II–V progression, which happens to be a very common one in music. As a matter of fact, in charts of progressions you will find sometimes the chords listed by Roman numeral instead of names, so that the player can put the song in whatever key suits him. Just to make this all clear, here is a bit of a progression with the chords properly marked:

(The progression above is a common one. The chords would normally be played in various inversions, but I have put them all in root position to make it easier for you to work out.)

Now, with the problem of nomenclature settled, we can begin to examine how chord progressions are put together. And the first thing you should know is that just as there are dissonant and consonant intervals, so there dissonant and consonant chords.

Generally speaking, major and minor chords are considered consonant. All others are called dissonant. Unfortunately, these terms are not really exact. In today's music we hear so many dominant 7ths, for example, that in some circumstances they may sound quite consonant. Therefore, it is probably wiser for us to say that some chords are less consonant, or more dissonant, than others. As a general rule we can say approximately this: major and minor triads are consonant; 7th chords are less consonant than simple major and minor triads; diminished and augmented chords are still less consonant; and the other chords, like 9ths, diminished 9ths, and so forth, are less consonant still.

However, there is really no strict rule you can apply. What seems more consonant to one ear may seem more dissonant to another. Nonetheless, the general rule is approximately correct: major and minor chords are consonant; all other chords are dissonant to one degree or another.

What consonance and dissonance have to do with chord progressions is this. A dissonant chord seems to the ear to be incomplete, unfinished. There is something a little out of whack about it, something that needs to be fixed or put back in order. The player or listener wants it put right; he wants the dissonance removed. In a word, he wants it to become consonant—or, as musicians put it, he wants the chord to *resolve*.

This need for resolution is one of the most important propelling forces in music. A dissonant chord resolves to a consonant chord, which then changes to another dissonant chord which must in turn be resolved. It is a pattern of tension and release, which is very much a part of life: you get hungry, and you eat, releasing the tension of hunger; you get frightened, and you run; you get angry, and you shout.

In the same way that the tensions you feel impel you to action, so the tensions in chords drive them toward resolution, sweeping the music along with them. Now, chord movement is not the only thing that impels music along. Things that happen in the melody help too, and so do rhythms. Again, not all Western music uses this movement from dissonance to consonance. In modern music—classical, jazz, or rock—there is sometimes so much dissonance that nothing ever resolves, in a strict sense.

Nonetheless, in most of the music with which you are familiar, there is some sort of dissonance–consonance movement, even if it comes in only periodically. And our problem now is: which chords resolve best to which other chords?

All chords are related to one degree or another. Some are very closely related: brothers and sisters, really. Others are more distantly related, like uncles and aunts. And still others are third cousins who only get together on rare occasions.

This family analogy of relationships is a little silly, I grant, but it gives a good idea of the thing. In looking at chords, we are going to try to find some ways of putting them in groups that belong together.

In putting things together in categories, you often find that there are several ways of grouping them. For example, a vegetable merchant could group his wares by color, so that beets, radishes, and tomatoes were together. Or he could do it by size, so that beets went with potatoes, and radishes with lima beans; or by price, so that all the expensive ones went together; or by whether they grew on vines or in the ground; or by the season they came in; or by first initials; or by . . . well, there is no need to go on. Quite obviously, you can categorize vegetables in many different ways.

The same thing can be done with chords. There are a number of ways of grouping them. But the interesting and fortunate fact is that no matter which method of categorizing you use, the results are approximately the same.

Then why bother with a number of ways of categorizing

chords? Why not use one and be done with it? The answer to that question goes back to that statement I made at the beginning of the book. Theory is not a set of rules for you to follow blindly, but a way of thinking about music that helps you to understand how it works. Therefore, if you know several ways in which chords can be grouped, you will know more about how music all joins together than if you know only one.

The Dominant–Tonic Relationship

Back in an earlier chapter I said that if you learn nothing else from this book, you should at least get a death grip on the dominant–tonic relationship. The strongest pull in chord movements is from the dominant to the tonic or, as we have it in our new notation, from the V chord to the I chord. Try it, and your ear will tell you the truth of it:

This relationship is even stronger when we use the dominant-7th chord—the V7—instead of the plain dominant-triad. Try it again:

The reasons why this chord movement is so strong and effective have to do with a number of things too complicated to get into here. Theorists aren't entirely sure why this relationship works so well, anyway. However, the ear knows that it is true. This re-

lationship appears at least once in nearly all of the music written
in the past three hundred years. Many pieces of music hardly
do more than move back and forth between the dominant 7th
and the tonic—the V7 and the I, to use proper notation. Children's
songs are likely to be based almost entirely on dominant–tonic
movements. So is a good deal of rock music and some of the simpler jazz music. Indeed, because the dominant–tonic progression
gives such a satisfying feeling of completeness, it almost inevitably
appears at the endings of musical pieces, especially in popular
music. This V–I progression is so common that it even has a
name—"perfect cadence." I simply cannot overemphasize the importance of the dominant–tonic relationship.

We have, then, a pair of extremely closely-related chords—any
chord, and its dominant, especially its dominant 7th. But if you
pause to think about it a minute, you can see that this relationship
works two ways. Every chord has a dominant to which it is closely
tied; but it is also the dominant of some other chord, to which
it is just as closely tied. C is the dominant of F; and F is the
dominant of Bb. Bb, as it happens, is the IV chord in F. Logically,
the chord of which another chord is the dominant is its IV chord.

We now have found a little family of three chords: a chord, its
dominant, and the chord it is the dominant of. Or to put it in our
new notation, the I chord, the IV chord, and the V chord. This
little family of I–IV–V is the closest-knit family in chords. Thousands upon thousands of songs have been written utilizing just
these three. As a matter of fact, the blues is nothing more or less
than a working out of the I–IV–V relationship. Here is the basic
blues pattern:

‖ I / / / | I / / / | I / / / | I7 / / / | IV / / / | IV / / / |

| I / / / | I / / / | V7 / / / | V7 / / / | I / / / | I / / / ‖

There are a number of variations on this blues pattern, but they all are essentially built on the I–IV–V relationship. This is certainly an important reason why the blues have had such a profound effect on all our contemporary music: the relationship is such a basic one.

The Circle of Fifths

But now we have to complete the logic. C is the dominant of F and F is the dominant of B♭; B♭ obviously has to be the dominant of some other chord, and it is: E♭. But then E♭ in turn must be the dominant of something else; and so forth. And if you take the trouble to work out this sequence of dominant–tonic relationships, you discover that they make a circle which runs through all keys and ends up back where it started, with C. This endless chain is called the Circle of Fifths. It looks like this:

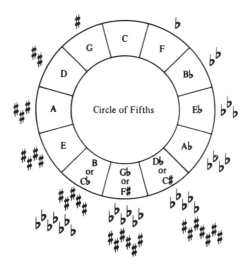

The Circle of Fifths has long been known and valued by musicians. It is something you simply should memorize. For one thing, as you will notice, the signatures for the keys travel in an orderly sequence around the Circle of Fifths. Begin with C, which has no sharps or flats in its signature. Traveling clockwise around the Circle you add one flat for each key; traveling counter-clockwise from C you add one sharp for each key. Once you know the Circle of Fifths you can find the right signature for any key in about three seconds.

More important, however, the Circle of Fifths tells us a great deal about chord relationships. Any three chords in a row on the Circle of Fifths make up a I–IV–V family—the I in the middle, the V to the right, the IV to the left. Thus, a tonic chord is always surrounded on the Circle of Fifths by its closest relations, its IV and V chords.

This fact logically suggests something else: the closer two chords are on the Circle of Fifths, the more closely they are related. Vice versa, the farther two chords are apart on the Circle of Fifths, the more distant they are. This is not merely theory. Try playing a sequence of two chords as far apart as you can get on the Circle of Fifths, and then compare it with a sequence of closer chords:

The first movement is between two chords directly opposite each other on the Circle of Fifths. The second is between chords adjacent to each other. Your ear should make the difference clear.

The Circle of Fifths is an extremely handy tool for you to have. It will help you time and time again both in making music and in playing it. It is one thing you really should get by heart.

8

Other Chord Relationships

THE CIRCLE OF FIFTHS is an exceedingly useful tool in helping composers put together sequences of chords. You can always move back and forth between adjacent I, IV, and V chords; you can always travel around it in a clockwise direction for a few chords; and you can skip around fairly easily in either direction to a chord two or three steps away in the Circle of Fifths—from an F to an E♭ or a G, for example.

But the Circle of Fifths is not the whole answer to chord movement. It is principally of use in dealing with major chords, and especially dominant 7ths. It doesn't always work out as well with minors, 9ths, and other types of chords. For example the Vm chord does not move nearly as easily to the I chord, or even to the Im chord, as the V7 does.

The Scale Family of Chords

We need another system of grouping chords to help us deal with minors, diminished chords, 9ths, and the rest. For this method we must return to the scale. As you remember, you can build chords by taking every other note from a scale, in this fashion:

And as you also remember, you don't have to begin with the tonic; you can begin with any note:

It should be clear, then, that out of any scale you can construct seven different triads. In a G-major scale, you can make triads on G, A, B, C, D, E, F♯. But if you stop to examine these chords you will see that they are not all majors. The triad made on the tonic—the I chord—is major. So is the IV chord and the V chord. But the II chord, built on A in the key of G, is minor. The III and VI are also minor. And the VII chord is diminished.

But if you start with a *minor* scale you will get different results. The I chord will be minor, the II will be diminished, and the III chord a major.

There is no special need to memorize which of these chords are majors and which are minors at this point, although if you go on studying music you will learn them. The point is this: no matter what type of scale you begin with, you can make a set of chords with some major, some minor, some diminished, and—in one rare instance—augmented. The chords built this way fall into a group because they are all made from the same seven notes —the notes from one scale. And this is so even if you continue on up the scale to make 7ths or 9ths, or anything else.

You can, then, make a perfectly acceptable chord progression by using only chords which can be made from the notes found in one scale. They will flow smoothly from one to the other in almost any order you use them in. And it should not surprise you to know that in Bach's time most music was written along these lines. The composers of that day felt that you ought to stick with the notes of the scale of the key you were in. To get variety, they would change key—but as long as they stayed in the same key they stuck fairly closely to the seven notes of one scale.

Working with this method of grouping chords gives some interesting results. For example, in the Circle of Fifths G and Bb are quite far apart. GM chord has a B in it, obviously jarring in the key of Bb. But in a Gm chord the B becomes a Bb. G-*minor* and Bb-*major* chords can be made from the same scale, and if you hear them in succession you will see that they are closely related:

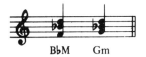

BbM   Gm

Similarly, B and C are almost as far apart as you can get on the Circle of Fifths. But a B-*diminished* chord can be made from a C-major scale, and it thus relates fairly closely to a CM chord.

Chords with Common Tones

We now have two methods of grouping chords: by the Circle of Fifths, and by the scales that they can be built from. But we still have some holes to fill. For instance, what about the chords FM and Fm? They are not in a dominant–tonic relationship, and they can't be built from the same scale, since one has an A in it and the other an A♭. Yet they are built on the same tonic: obviously they are in some kind of relationship.

We could make a rule saying that all chords with the same tonic are a group, but there is a more useful idea. That is: chords which have notes in common are related. FM and Fm have two notes the same: F and C. They are closely related, as your ear will tell you.

If you experiment with this theory, however, your ear will tell you that, generally speaking, one common note is not enough: chords need to have two or more notes in common to sound related. CM and A♭M both have C's in them, but if you try them out in succession you will see that they are not at all close.

The tonic does not have to be one of the common tones. Below are some groups of triads with different tonics which have two notes in common:

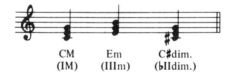

CM   Em   C♯dim.
(IM)   (IIIm)   (♭IIdim.)

The chords in the example above are all triads. When we deal with 7th chords the list increases. For example, we saw earlier that GM and B♭M are not close on the Circle of Fifths, and can't be made from the same scale. To bring them closer together, we turned the GM into a Gm. But there is another stunt: turn the GM into a G7 chord. The 7th is F. G7 and B♭M have two notes in common, F and D:

The chords become much more closely related. Composers recognize this fact and use this combination of BbM–G7, or I–V17, very frequently. Here, then, is another group of chords with two notes in common:

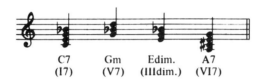

We now have three different ways of finding how closely related any two chords are: by the Circle of Fifths; by the scales they are derived from; and by their common tones. And the next question we must ask is: are these rules consistent?

Yes, they are. You will find more often than not that two chords which relate closely by one method will relate closely by another. For example, FM and Am have two common tones; they can also be derived from the same scale. FM and CM can be made from the same scale, and they are next to each other on the Circle of Fifths. You will not find two rules for every case, but you will find them often.

More important, are there any cases when one rule says two chords are distant relations, and another rule says they are close? No; but there is one chord relationship which doesn't seem to fit very well into any of our categories. A major chord and its diminished version can't be made from the same scale, aren't in a dominant–tonic relationship, and have only one note in common. We had better say, then, that a diminished chord relates to its tonic major and minor, and let it go at that. (It doesn't relate too well to its augmented brother, however.)

But I must again repeat: music is not black scratches on paper, it is sounds in the ear. None of these rules is exact and perfectly consistent, like the rules of mathematics. In working with music you can't simply follow the rules blindly. You must use your ear, your common sense, and your imagination. The point of studying theory is not to give you rules that you must obey, but to give you a sense of how music works, a way of seeing how all of this mass of sound can be worked up into patterns.

Making Chord Progressions

We have, in any case, now established some relationships which tell us which chords follow easily from any given chord. By using these rules you should now be able to put together without much difficulty a smooth-flowing chord progression. But is it enough merely to make a chord progression move smoothly along?

Yes, sometimes; but not always. If you are dealing with a type of music where most of the interest is centered on rhythmic patterns or a powerful melodic line, such as jazz, a simple, fairly straightforward chord progression, using a few basic chords, is often adequate. Some of the best jazz ever played was made on the I–IV–V changes of the blues. Rock players, in fact, often work with even simpler changes. A great deal of rock alternates between a minor chord and its dominant 7th: Im–V7–Im–V7, etc., for minutes at a time.

I want to make it clear that a chord progression doesn't have to be complicated in order to be good or useful. But obviously, an interesting chord progression is more than merely smooth-flowing. It has variety and imagination. It has some sort of logic to it. And it may even have a kind of drama to it.

These words *variety, logic, drama* are not easy to pin down. But then, music is never easy to pin down in words, and these words help to make the point that music is made by human beings with minds and feeling, not by a computer. I may not be able to explain to you how to put "imagination" into music; but you know what I mean by the term.

Even though there are no hard and fast rules for lining up chords in a progression, there are some tips which are helpful. Here are some ideas worth your thinking about:

(1) Not all music begins and ends on a tonic chord, but the largest percentage of the music with which you are familiar does. A beginning composer is well-advised to begin and end on major triads of the key his piece is in until he grows more familiar with chord patterns.

(2) It is easier to work in major keys than in minor keys; but of course you can—and should—use minor chords in a major key, and vice versa.

(3) Keep in mind the idea of dissonant–consonant tension and release. Music that is being driven along by powerful rhythms or cascading melodies may not need dissonant–consonant resolutions to make it move, but they are nonetheless never wrong.

(4) The Circle of Fifths is exceedingly useful. It is never a bad idea to travel around it for a few chords. Remember that the dominant 7th makes an even stronger relationship to the tonic than the plain dominant. A good trick is to make a major triad into a dominant 7th, resolve it to its tonic, and then make its tonic, in turn, into a dominant 7th: C—C7—F—F7—B♭—B♭7, etc. However, if you stick with the Circle of Fifths for too long at a stretch the music will become predictable and, thus, boring. You can go around the Circle of Fifths counterclockwise, too, but the music doesn't flow as easily.

(5) To give variety to a sequence of chords from the Circle of Fifths, find substitutes which can be fitted in for one or two chords

along the line. Suppose, for example, you have this sequence: G7–C7–F7–B♭. A Dm could be used in place of the C7, for it has two notes in common with the chords on either side of it.

(6) Vary the amount of time given to each chord. If your chords have been changing at the beginning of each measure, break the monotony occasionally by changing more often, or at some other place in the measures.

(7) Look for some sort of internal logic. Sometimes you can work chords out so that one voice goes down a scale, or moves along in half steps. One quite common progression that uses the latter device is the following, which I've put in the key of C here:

| FM | Fm | CM | D7 | G7 | CM |
| (IVM) | (IVm) | (IM) | (V7) | (V7) | (IM) |

(8) Use distantly related chords for variety and color, but use them sparingly. Too many distant chords coming along one after another will make the music seem abrupt, jerky, and senseless.

(9) One good general approach to composing is to start with the tonic, move away from it for a period, and then start moving back toward it again. This idea gives music a certain logic and even drama, but allows for infinite variety. A good deal of music of all types is put together this way.

None of the ideas above are rules that must be strictly followed, or followed at all. They are merely suggestions for ways of working. Hopefully, you will come up with ideas of your own as you see how chord progressions are put together. One last suggestion: in working out chord patterns, be simple. There is nothing wrong with a simple chord progression, if it works.

9

Melody

WE ARE NOW about two-thirds of the way through this book and so far we haven't even mentioned what may be the most important part of music. That is melody. Melody is where music begins. It is the part of music we learn first as children. A song is melody. Melody is what we sing in the shower or whistle while we work. In ancient times melody was about all the music man had, and in some cultures this is still true today.

It would seem, then, that in studying music we ought to begin with melody, instead of chords. Yet the reason for doing it the other way around is embodied in what I said two chapters back about playing chords as melody. This is an important idea, and I want to go over it again.

We commonly think of chords as several notes played simultaneously. But if you have ever studied the piano a little, you know that you can play a chord as an arpeggio—that is, play the notes one after another in quick succession. An arpeggio is still a chord. Now play the arpeggio slower, and then slower still. Somewhere along the line the notes become distinctly separate, and you have melody.

But do you have melody instead of a chord? No. You have a chord arranged as melody. The best way to think of chords, then, is as groups of related notes which can be played either together or one after another. That is, you can "express" or "state" a chord melodically as well as chordally.

Let's go a step further. In playing an arpeggio, you usually start with the bottom note and run up the chord playing the notes in order. But there is no special reason for doing this. The chord will still sound like the same chord if you start at the top and run downward. In fact, it will sound like the same chord if you start in the middle and play the notes in any order you chose. A GM chord, thus, can be played as melody in a variety of different ways:

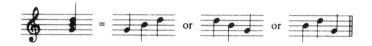

And now let's go another step. As you remember, you can double notes in chords, or omit them; and logically, you can do the same thing when you play the chord melodically:

GM
(with tonic doubled)

GM
(with 5th omitted)

In the end we are going to say that there are a vast number of different ways of playing a chord melodically. Indeed, since nearly all melody is an expression of a chord pattern, there are as many ways of playing chords as there are melodies—and that is an enormous number.

Since there are so many thousands of ways of expressing a single chord it would almost seem that you could put down at random a group of notes and end up with something. And as a matter of fact, you very nearly can. Any four or five notes picked out of mid-air and arranged in random fashion are likely to express one chord or another. It isn't inevitable, though: it is very difficult to add up some combinations of notes and get a chord. But more often than not, a group of notes will sound like one chord or another. That being the case, why can't you just write a melody that suits you and figure out what the chords are later?

You can, of course. This is a perfectly legitimate way to go about composing, one that many famous songwriters have used. However, a musician still has to know what chord any sequence of notes is expressing, and perhaps more important, he must be able to find a melody that expresses a given chord. In other words, he has to know how melody relates to a chord progression. He has to know this in the first place so he can find the right chords to accompany a melody he has written or heard somewhere. In the second place, in many types of music today all the musician has to work from is chords. He is given a chord chart and is expected to provide a melody. This is what the improvising jazz or rock player is doing—making melody to fit predetermined chords. Or, as an arranger, he may have to work out variations on the melody of a song but keep the original chord progression. A musician, even an amateur or beginner, must know how chords and melody relate. In point of fact, a great deal of what you have learned so far has been precisely for this purpose.

Non-Chord Tones

The rules are not hard and fast. Common sense is a big help, and in the end, the best guide always has to be the ear. But there are some guidelines that help.

The first rule, obviously, is that if all, or most, of the notes in a phrase of music belong to a given chord, melody is obviously expressing that chord:

Auxiliary tone

Above is a very common, little jazz figure. It is clearly an FM chord, even though the second note is a D, because all the other notes in the figures are F, A, and C, which add up to an FM chord. A note like the D, which is just a tone or a half tone from a chord tone, which is approached by this chord tone, and which then returns to it, is called an *auxiliary* tone, or an *upper neighbor*. (A *lower neighbor* is just the opposite.)

Here is another type of non-chord tone:

Appoggiatura

The chord expressed is clearly FM again. The A♭ suggests that the chord might be an Fm, but the ear won't hear it that way. For one thing, there are two A's and only one A♭. For another—and this is the most important reason—the ear is going to hear that little beginning A♭ as a kind of lead-in note. "Lead-in" notes of this kind are called *appoggiaturas,* which comes from the Italian word meaning to "lean on." Appoggiaturas always come on the strong beat.

Here is yet another type of non-chord tone:

Passing tone

This figure states a GM chord quite strongly, despite the A, which is not in a GM chord. The music just seems to be "passing through" the A, and as a matter of fact, musicians call a tone like this, which comes in between two chord tones, a *passing tone*. Here's another example of a passing tone:

Passing tones

In this example there are no less than three passing tones, but beginning and ending on C, and including both G and E, the melody is distinctly built out of a CM chord, as your ear will tell you.

Emphasizing Chord Tones

In the foregoing examples, we made the chord clear by making sure that most of the notes in the melodic figure belonged to the chord. However, it is entirely possible to make chords when a majority of the notes are not chord tones. The way to do it is simply to emphasize the chord notes. And the simplest, most common way of doing this is to put the chord tones on the strong beats in a measure. As you may already know, in $\frac{4}{4}$ time the first and third beats are strong, the second and fourth beats are weak. In

$\frac{3}{4}$ the first beat is strong. In $\frac{6}{8}$ the first and fourth beats are the strong ones:

If you keep the chord tones on the strong beats you will get a distinct impression of the chord, regardless of what notes fall on the other beats:

Chord tones

In the example above the notes on the strong beats are F, D, A, F, D, which spell Dm, and the ear will distinctly hear the melody as expressing a Dm chord.

The same effect works when you have an even more crowded measure:

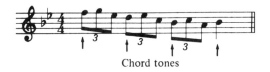

Chord tones

The notes that fall on the beginning of each beat—the downbeat —are much more strongly emphasized than the notes which fall off the beat. In this case the notes on downbeats spell a B♭M chord.

Notes on the strong beats of a measure are invariably emphasized unless some other factor comes into play. But there are, of
course, other ways to emphasize notes. You can easily shift the
emphasis to the weak beats by having them played louder or
attacked more sharply, or giving them to more powerful instruments—trumpets, say, instead of flutes. Common sense will suggest
to you ways that this can be done. The important thing to remember is that whatever notes are emphasized will be the ones the ear
uses to spell out the chord.

In jazz, for example, players quite deliberately, in $\frac{4}{4}$ time, keep
the emphasis off the first and third beat. In fact, jazz players are
likely to throw the emphasis off the beat altogether. The notes
then get their emphasis from the way the players accent, or attack them, or hold them out. Here is a typical jazz figure:

The notes on the first and third beats are F and D, suggesting a
Dm or a B♭M chord, perhaps. The other two notes fall off the
beat entirely, but they are clearly the most important ones in the
measure. (In actual playing a jazz musician would probably accent them, as well.) They are E and C, suggesting a C chord; and
that is what the ear will hear.

In the example above we did not have the full three notes of
a triad. This suggests that just as you can omit notes from a chord
sounded together, so you can omit notes from a chord played melodically. As a matter of fact, more likely than not a melody will
tend to suggest chords, rather than spell them out completely, like
this:

It is quite obvious that the above melody is suggesting a C7 chord, even though the 5th, G, never appears. There is really nothing else it can be. However, the minute we begin talking about omissions we run into some problems, because any two notes a third apart can belong to several chords. Take, for example, the notes G and B♭, which make a minor 3rd. They can be found in E♭M, Gm, one of the diminished-7th chords, and two or three others. A melody employing only the two notes of a third, thus, is ambiguous. You need some other factors in order to establish what chord is meant.

Two notes the interval of a 5th apart, however, establish a tonality most firmly. The notes C and G can be found together only in two chords: CM and Cm. Two notes a 5th apart, thus, emphatically state tonality. C and G won't tell you whether the chord is a major or minor, but they will say C chord, no matter which note is played first or which one is higher. (Actually C and G can both be found in various of the G11 chords, but if just those two notes are played, the ear will always hear them as part of a C triad, not as part of a G11 chord.)

Using strong 5ths, then, is another sound way to express a chord:

In this example the strong 5th of the first two notes so emphatically insist on a C chord that even though the other notes are scattered around considerably, the effect of C will be felt.

Another way two notes of a triad can express a whole chord is through their scales. Take this example:

The notes D and F fall on the strong beats. But D and F are found in Dm, BbM, D diminished, and G7, just to name a few. Which one will the ear hear? The clue is the Eb, which is not found in any D or G major scale. It is, however, found in a Bb, scale, and the ear will thus tend to hear the D and F as the 3rd and 5th of a BbM chord. But if we make the Eb into an E, we will now hear a different chord, probably a Dm, although a G7 is possible.

A G7 is possible because of those other factors I mentioned a moment ago. All of the examples we have been looking at in this chapter are quite short—much shorter than melodies usually are. The ear has a memory, and everything that has gone before has an effect on how anything is heard. Suppose the little fragment in the last example had been preceded by a clear GM chord. It would then quite likely be heard as a G7 instead of a BbM. And if it had been preceded by an A7 it would almost certainly be heard as a Dm, despite the Eb. A7 is the dominant of Dm. The ear so much expects a dominant 7th to be followed by its tonic that it would insist on hearing a Dm. Indeed, if it had been preceded by a strongly stated Cm chord, the D and F might even be heard as the 9th and 11th of the same Cm chord, or perhaps simply as passing tones. (I say Cm instead of CM, because the E♭ belongs in a Cm chord, not to a CM one.)

As you can see, then, there is nothing hard and fast about the rules that relate chords and melody. Different people can hear things different ways at different times. Here is one interesting example:

I grew up during the big swing-band era when the 6th chord was used constantly. My ear will hear this as a B♭6; I will have a clear sense of B♭ being the tonic. My sons, however, have grown up in the rock era, when m7 chords are very common. They will hear this chord as Gm7, with just as clear a sense of a G tonality. And, as a matter of fact, composers quite often build this kind of ambiguity into music. The uncertainty can be quite interesting; after all, there is no reason why every bit of melody *must* belong to one chord or another, although of course usually the ear insists on it.

Accompanying Chords

For the sake of simplicity I have been talking about music as if it were played all alone, like a solo on a flute. As a practical matter, however, melody rarely comes this way today, except when you whistle in the shower. It almost always comes with some sort of accompaniment. It may be the harmonies provided by the altos, tenors, and basses in a chorus. It may be the piano and bass of a jazz rhythm-section, or the bass and rhythm guitar of a rock group.

It could be the soft chords of a big-band saxophone section playing underneath the lead trumpet. It could be the left hand of the pianist chopping out chords while his right hand plays the melody. And this fact gives us something more to think about in the relationship of chords and melody. Take this example:

These notes, A, C, F, could in theory be part of several different chords. They could be all of an FM triad. They could be 3rd, 5th, and minor 7th of a Dm7. They could be the 5th, major 7th, and 9th of a Bb9 chord. But if played alone and unaccompanied, the ear will almost certainly hear them as spelling out an FM chord, because the ear prefers to hear things the simplest way.

But—suppose while these notes are being played a jazz rhythm-section is hammering BbM chords. The situation is now altered considerably. The notes simply have to be heard as the 5th, 7th, and 9th of a BbM9. (There are exceptional cases when they would be heard as something else, but they are rare and for advanced study.) Thus, if you can get your chords stated firmly enough outside the melody, you can force the melody to sound like the parts of any chords you want. This is something that jazz musicians, especially bop musicians, do all the time. In improvising, bop musicians use enormous numbers of diminished 9ths, 7ths, and diminished 5ths. They count on the rhythm section to make plain the meaning they intend the notes to have.

What it almost comes down to is that melodically you can run together any sequence of notes and the ear will hear them as part of something. Almost—but not quite. A highly trained listener,

such as an experienced jazz improviser, can hear long strings of
11ths, diminished 5ths, and diminished 9ths for what they are—
or what they are intended to be, in any case. But to inexperienced
listeners, the effect is bound to be incomprehensible. They can't
hear how the notes are related. The music doesn't make any sense
to them, and they turn away in boredom. Indeed, even many
trained musicians can lose track of what's happening in the music
if the melody is too rich in 9ths, 11ths, and altered notes. As a
general rule, then, whether you are improvising or writing melody,
you should keep coming back to touch base with the chords. Most
people today have no trouble hearing 7ths properly, and they can
usually handle major 9ths if they are not faced with too many. But
11ths, diminished 9ths, and diminished 5ths should be used with
care. (The 13th will be heard as a 6th, with which audiences today
are quite familiar.) An untrained listener can cope with a diminished 5th if there is a tonic and a 3rd somewhere in the vicinity.
But too much ranging around in the upper parts of the chord, and
you'll simply turn him off.

10

Voice-Leading

Today much of our music is instrumental, but up until two hundred years ago or so, much of the music which people heard was vocal. Part of the reason for this was that many of the instruments of early times were not very good. They were often far out of tune, had limited ranges, and were difficult to play. You could make much better music with the human voice. As a consequence music theorists tended to think in terms of the voice.

One of the major problems they faced was which notes to give to which singers. Because of omissions, doublings, and inversions, there were many different ways of arranging vocal parts of the chord progressions moved along.

That is to say, would the altos take the 3rd of a given chord? Would the basses take the 5th? And so forth. Working these questions out came to be called "voice-leading." (Among popular musicians the term "voicing" is usually used, although "voice-leading" is more proper.) In medieval times voice-leading was a fairly simple matter. But as the triad developed, and as four-part harmony came along, with the notes spread out among sopranos, altos, tenors, and basses, the art of voice-leading became exceedingly complex. Here, for example, are several different ways of moving a C7 to an FM:

Some of the voice-leading in the example above is good, some is bad—perhaps it would be better to say that there is some which is better than others. If you try them out your ear will fairly well tell you which voice-leading works the best. However, you don't have to depend on your ear to help. If any part of music has been over-theorized, it is the whole matter of voice-leading. There are scores of rules, which advanced students of music study endlessly. Voice-leading is probably the one aspect of music in which a deaf person could get good results just by following the rules. In my opinion far too much time is spent in theory courses on voice-leading which could more profitably be spent on other subjects—rhythm and melody, for example.

The reason why so much theory has been developed around the subject of voice-leading has to do with the way music was composed in the past. Today, songwriters and, to some extent, composers of classic music, begin with a chord progression, or a melody, or work out both together. The way the parts are arranged is figured out later. In earlier times, however, composers were more likely to start with a melody, and then write lines of music for the basses, tenors, and altos that would make good harmonic sense. The chord progression was allowed to be whatever resulted from the harmonies. The idea was that if you followed the rules for voice-leading, the chord progression would turn out to be a good one. Indeed, composers sometimes would simply write four lines of music that flowed along in good harmonies, and the melody would be whatever ended up on the top line. Sometimes the idea of a "chord progression" didn't get into it at all. This way of working was responsible for some of the finest music we have and is still a perfectly good way of going about composing. Today, however, much of our music, especially jazz and rock, isn't "voiced" at all in the traditional sense. Modern musicians are much more often required to begin by working out a chord progression then making a melody that fits the chords, and only later on—if ever—arranging the final result for a choir of instruments, in say, a big band backing up a singer. And this, of course, is the reason why I have organized this book the way it is.

But even though voice-leading is less important to musicians than it once was, it still is an indispensible technique. There is still a great deal of choral music today—not only for church choirs and community chorus, but for the ever-present singing groups on television. March music has to be voiced, background music for singers and dancers has to be voiced, all of the music you hear in television and radio commercials has to be voiced, big-band jazz has to be voiced, and of course many new classical works are voiced. As a matter of fact, even in jam sessions or jazz rehearsals a section leader may play a figure to which other members of the group are expected to work out harmonies instantaneously, as they are playing it. An understanding of at least the basic rules of voice-leading is essential to doing this.

The basic idea in voice-leading is to make the music flow smoothly and logically through the chord progression, so that the listener gets an impression of a natural movement of sound. Even if your chord progression is a smooth one, it can sound awkward and jerky if badly voiced. A series of chords in root position, for example, is almost always going to sound like a catalogue of

chords put out for display, as you can hear in the following example:

The first principle of good voice-leading is to move each part to
the nearest convenient note. In general, the notes should move as
little as possible:

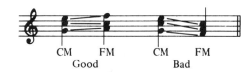

In the above example, the two chords have a C in common. If
possible, we want to work things out so that the same voice will
sing the C in both chords. Not only will this make for a smoother
movement from one chord to the next, but it will help to tie the
two chords together so that the ear senses them as related, as two
parts of the same thing. Also, there is an E in the C chord, and an
F a half step away from it in the F chord. The ear is going to want
very strongly for the E, not the G or the C, to resolve to the F, because the distance is so short. It just seems to the ear "righter,"
more natural. This leaves the G, which need move only a tone to
A, to complete the movement.

This basic principle of making each voice move as little as possible is a key one in voice-leading. As we get a little further along
in this chapter we will come across a number of exceptions, but
the principle is still a good one.

The principle does more than help us assign the chord notes to the various voices. If you think about it for a minute, you will find that all at once it makes clear why certain chords are much closer to others. Let's look at the famous dominant-7th–tonic relationship.

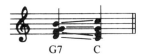

G7   C

As you can see in the example above, to move the G7 to CM in this particular inversion requires the B to move a half step up to the C, the F a half step down to E, and the D a whole step down to C; the G stands still. There is no effort, no jumping around. Everything in the G7 chord just shifts a little bit, and presto, you have a CM.

But there is another factor at work in this particular relationship. Any time the major 7th of the key you are in turns up in the melody, or even in the harmony, it is going to pull strongly upward toward the tonic. The M7 does not invariably move up to the tonic. For example, if it comes *after* the tonic, you have the first two notes of a scale going down, and the musical line can just as easily keep on going down to the 6th. Nonetheless, the movement of the 7th of the scale up to the tonic is one of the strongest in music, and it helps to explain why the dominant so readily moves to the tonic.

This, then, is the basic rule: move each note as little as possible to get to the next chord. Now you can see why doublings, inversions, and omissions are so necessary. Without them, you could never have smooth voice-leading.

There are, however, many occasions when this basic rule has to be broken, or at least bent a little. As I have said, there are scores of rules for achieving good effects in voice-leading—far too many for us to deal with in this book. I am going to give, therefore, only a few basic ones. Using these alone you will be able to write fairly good harmonic lines. Here, then, are some rules for voice-leading:

(1) The top line is almost always the melody—not because I say so, but because the listener will normally hear whatever is on top as the melody. There is no way around this.

(2) The lines of music in any of the parts should not jump wildly around from place to place, because it makes them hard to sing or even play correctly. The easiest, smoothest movement to make is the next note up or down the scale. There is always a good deal of scalewise movement in properly voiced music. Half steps are easy, too. The next easiest movements are 3rds and 5ths. Leaps larger than 5ths usually can be avoided. Large intervals are hard for singers and players of wind instruments to hit in tune. Tritones and major 7ths are especially hard intervals to sing and should never be used except in cases of dire emergency.

(3) In any sort of voice-leading or arranging you have to take into account the ranges of the voices or instruments for which you are writing. In the back of this book there is a chart of the ranges of the major instruments (see Appendix C).

(4) In general, the notes in the bottom parts can be spaced out more widely than the notes in the upper parts.

The first arrangement of the C chord will sound a little more secure than the second version. When the intervals on the top of

the chord are **larger** than the bottom ones, the ear seems to feel
that the chord is top-heavy.

(5) The firmest, most solid arrangement of voices has the tonic
on the top and bottom:

This arrangement is an excellent one for the final chord of a song,
or any place where the music is coming to a stop.

(6) Parallel 5ths and octaves should be avoided. Parallel 3rds
are acceptable. You get parallel movement when two voices stay
the same interval apart as they move from one chord to the next:

In the example above, the bottom two notes of the first chord, C
and G, stay a 5th apart as they move down to Bb and F. Again:

In this example the top and bottom notes of the first chord are
C's an octave apart; and they move to D's an octave apart, making
parallel octaves. The reason why parallel 5ths and octaves should
be avoided is that they give chord movement the same chunky

sound you get by playing in succession several chords in root position. Parallel 3rds, however, are not only acceptable, but standard practice:

(7) The above example not only contains parallel 3rds, it also contains something you try to put into voice-leading: contrary motion. You get contrary motion when two parts move in opposite directions, so that they are getting either farther apart or closer together:

Contrary motion is valuable. However, you obviously can't have all four voices moving in opposite directions, unless some of them are coming straight off the page at you. Therefore, since you want to avoid parallel 5ths and octaves, if you have to choose, use parallel motion in the 3rds, contrary motion in the 5ths and octaves, if you have them.

(8) The rules for doubling, omitting, and inverting chords, which you learned back in Chapter 6, apply to voice-leading as well. As a matter of fact, they were specifically worked out for solving problems in voice-leading. If you don't have them firmly in your mind, look them over again.

(9) In practice, you will often have to move one of the voices a 4th or a 5th. The best place to make big skips is in the bass. If

you take a look at the bass line in a book of four-part harmonies you will see how often this is done. In a lot of simple voice-leading practices, the bass moves from the tonic of one chord to the tonic of the next, chord after chord.

(10) All of the above rules can and should be broken from time to time. As a matter of fact, quite often you will find yourself in situations where you have to break one rule in order to keep another. Think of the rules I have given you not as laws, but as guidelines for what will sound well in the ear. In the end, the ear is the final referee for everything in music.

Minor Harmonies

Until now I have held off talking about certain problems that arise in dealing with minor scales and their chords. Now we must get to them. At the beginning of this book, you will remember, I said that there were several minor scales. The one we took note of was the *natural* minor:

Natural Minor

As you can see, you flat the 3rd, 6th, and 7th of a major scale to get a natural minor. But now we have a problem. Let's make a dominant chord from this natural minor-C scale:

The dominant of this natural minor scale on C is not GM, but Gm. And if you listen to this particular sort of dominant-tonic movement, you will discover that it doesn't have much propulsive power:

The reason why it lacks much movement is because the B♭—the leading tone—is a whole tone away from the C. It doesn't lead the ear up the scale to the C the way a B will. It tends to want, in fact, to move the other way. So now we know something new: a dominant-*minor* chord doesn't necessarily move to the tonic. In the dominant–tonic relationship, the dominant must be a major chord, even when the tonic is a minor. GM to Cm will work; Gm to CM won't work as a dominant.

When composers began to discover this effect, they decided that the simplest way around it was to make a change in the minor scale. They made the 7th a major instead of a minor 7th. So they created a second type of minor scale:

Harmonic Minor

They called this scale the *harmonic* minor, because it was invented to make harmonic movements work better. But now, having gotten rid of one problem, they discovered that they had created another. If you look at the harmonic-minor scale in the example above you will find that between the 6th and the 7th there is not just a whole

step, but a step and a half. When the scale was being used merely
to make chords, this big jump didn't matter; but when it was used
for making melody, this extra skip disturbed the ear. It was like
missing a step in a flight of stairs.

To solve the problem, musicians invented still another minor
scale:

They called this scale the melodic minor, because it was to be used
in melodies. This scale now has no steps longer than a whole
tone, and the 7th is a major. Two problems were solved; but now
there was a third. Only the 3rd of the melodic minor was flatted.
Everywhere else the scale was identical to its tonic major. Most of
the special minor sound was gone. But theorists realized one more
thing, which was that a melody needs a major 7th only when it is
going *upwards* toward the tonic. When it is coming *down* from the
tonic, it doesn't matter whether the 7th is major or minor, since
it isn't supposed to be pushing the music toward the tonic above it
anyway. And so they developed one more rule. Going up, use the
melodic minor; coming down, use the natural minor. Or to put it
another way, in the melodic minor, when going up, only the 3rd is
flatted; when coming down, 3rd, 6th, and 7th are flatted:

Melodic Minor

As a practical matter, at this point in your studies, what this really means is that when you are going upwards to the tonic in either major or minor, use a major 7th, and always use major dominant-7th chords, regardless of whether you are in a major or minor key.

Now, to see how voice-leading works in practice, let's look at the opening phrase from one of the most lasting and popular pieces of music ever written, the hymn called *Doxology,* or *Old Hundredth:*

GM   GM   DM   Em   Bm   Em   DM   GM

The first thing to notice is that the chord progression in this phrase begins and ends on the tonic GM, and never travels too far around the Circle of Fifths. Secondly, all of the chords can be built from a G-major scale. Thirdly, all of them have notes in common with GM, and with nearly all of the other chords in the progression as well. The four chords here, clearly, are a closely knit little group. They are, in chord notation, IM, IIIm, VIm, and VM, and you will find this group working together time and time again in music.

Now, notice that in every case the bass has the tonic of the chord. This is a very common practice and gives the music a sure solidity, which you especially want in a hymn. It is not very imaginative, to be sure, but it also puts large skips of 4ths and 5ths in the bass, which is certain to make closer voice-leading in the upper parts easier.

With the tonics in the bass, however, you can't simply give the tenor the 5ths, for that will give you a whole series of parallel 5ths. Instead, this part has been skillfully arranged so that it always moves up and down by scale steps, most of the time a 3rd away from the melody, which is also moving by scale steps.

Now look at the alto part. It moves only twice during the whole phrase. The part is no doubt somewhat dull to sing, but remaining stable as it does through several chord changes in a row, it helps to tie the music tightly together.

There are no parallel 5ths or octaves in this short fragment. There is contrary motion in almost every movement. There are no skips larger than a 5th, and only one as big as that. The only one of our rules that is broken is that in several instances the upper parts are more widely spaced than the lower ones. Taken as a whole, this opening phrase from *Old Hundredth* is a marvelous piece of machinery. It is quite simple, and yet it works beautifully. The parts move together in a fashion that the ear finds both pleasing and logical. And people have enjoyed listening to it for over four hundred years. When something lasts that long, it must have something to it. And this, in turn, suggests that the reason why we study music theory is because it works.

Up to this point we have been looking at ways to voice four-part music. Music doesn't always come in four parts, however. Symphony orchestras normally have three trumpets. Big dance bands usually have five saxophones and eight or ten brasses which are sometimes voiced together.

Voice-leading for groups of any size is based on the theory of four-part voice-leading. For smaller groups, essentially, you omit one note according to the rules for omitting we looked at earlier. For larger groups, you double one or more of the notes. However, there is more to be said about voicing for larger groups than that. In practice, what often happens, if the group is a large one like the clarinet section of a school marching-band, is that several instruments play the same part. Regular four-part voice-leading is used. However, a fifth or sixth voice in, say, the saxophone section of a jazz band allows the composer to add 9ths, 11ths, and what-not, and this is what usually happens. The rules for using the higher parts of the chords follow the lines laid out for the other notes.

Voice-leading can be a lot like playing chess or working out crossword puzzles. There are usually a number of choices you can make and still stay within the rules. To develop facility at voice-leading requires a lot of practice. It is something you do over and over. But there is hardly anything you can do which will give you a better grip on music. Once you have done a lot of voice-leading much of the theory in this book will become second nature to you, something you will manage as easily as you do words.

11

Rhythm

RHYTHM IS ONE of those subjects in music theory that nobody talks about very much, mostly because they don't know what to say about it. Everything you can say about rhythm seems to be either too simple or too complicated. Yet it is vital to music in all senses of the word. *Vital* means "full of life," and it is rhythm that fills music with life. You can make interesting and exciting music with rhythm alone; but it is hard to make any kind of music at all without it.

To be sure, there are kinds of music which have rather vague beats. The Gregorian chants, which I talked about earlier, lack regular pulsing rhythms: the notes just come meandering along taking their own good time. But no music is *totally* without a beat, and most of the music with which you are familiar has a most strict and exact rhythmic pulse.

We ordinarily think of rhythm as something which is supplied by a "rhythm section"—the drums in a marching band, the rhythm guitar in a rock group, the bass, drums, and piano in a dance band. But as you are of course aware, a line of music, either melody or a series of chords, supplies its own rhythmic pulse. Sing *Happy Birthday* and the beat is there, locked into the music itself. You can't always tell what the musical pulse of a piece of music is by looking at the score, but you can always feel it the minute the music is played.

The pulse of a piece of music is established by the beginnings, and to a lesser extent the endings, of notes. This beat can be changed or modified to some extent by the way we accent notes, but basically it is the beginning of the notes that sets the pulse. If, for example, you string out a number of notes of equal value one after another, you will create a distinct musical pulse:

 etc.

These notes each have equal value, and so long as you play them that way they will produce the effect of a rhythmic pulse, no matter how fast or slow you make it. A bass drum in a marching band or the electric bass in a rock group hammers out this kind of fundamental music to make a pulse. A rhythmic pulse, then, is established when all, or most, of the notes in a melody are the same length. But of course any music consisting entirely of notes of equal length would grow relentless after awhile, like a Chinese water-torture. Improvisers and composers, therefore, mix notes of varying lengths into their compositions:

In the example above, I have added interest to the first bit of melody by shortening some of the notes and lengthening others. But now a question arises. In the first example we had eight equal notes, which gave us a rhythmic pulse of eight beats. In this new bit of melody we have ten notes of three different lengths. Are there eight beats in this bit of music? Sixteen? Or only four? In other words, do the quarter notes each get a beat? Or the eighth notes? Or does the half note get one beat?

The fact of the matter is that there is no way to tell unless a time signature is put in. (Unless, of course, you hear the music.) You should know how to read time signatures by this point, but just for the record, I'll explain. A time signature is made up of two numbers one on top of the other, like a fraction. The top number tells the number of beats in a measure. The bottom number tells what kind of note gets one beat. In $\frac{3}{4}$ time, for instance:

3=three beats in a measure

4=a quarter note gets one beat.

The other commonly used time signatures are $\frac{4}{4}$, which is also written as a C; $\frac{2}{2}$, which usually is written ¢ and is called "cut time"; $\frac{2}{4}$; and $\frac{6}{8}$, which is played six beats to a measure, an eighth note getting one beat at slow tempos; and two beats in a measure, a dotted quarter-note getting one beat at fast tempos, especially marches.

Now, let's put a time signature into our little bit of melody:

The $\frac{4}{4}$ signature says that the four quarter-notes each get a beat. Our little figure, thus, is eight beats long.

But what about this:

I have changed the time signature to cut time, or $\frac{2}{2}$. Now a half note gets one beat—and there are only two beats to a measure. Suppose we set our rhythmic pulse going at just half the speed as we used for the figure when it was $\frac{4}{4}$. It will take exactly the same length of time to play the figure with either time signature. What difference, then, does it make whether we play anything in $\frac{4}{4}$ or $\frac{2}{2}$?

As a practical matter, musicians often play music written in cut time as if it were written in $\frac{4}{4}$, putting in twice as many beats so that the music comes out right. A good deal of popular music is marked ¢ on the sheet music, but it is invariably played in $\frac{4}{4}$. Nonetheless, there is subtle difference in the way the music comes out. There will be very tiny differences in the attack, exactly how long the notes are held out, the accents, and so forth. The players will hardly be conscious of making these differences, but they will be there.

The above is a second way a rhythmic pulse can be established: by the subtleties of playing which may not be visible in the score. Here is a third way:

In the above example some of the beats have been divided into unequal parts. The little melody could still be played in ¢ or in $\frac{8}{8}$, with an eighth note getting one beat, but there is going to be a strong tendency for the ear to hear an unequal figure as a single beat, unless it is played quite slowly. Here's another example:

The figure with the little 3 over it is called a triplet—three notes in one beat. (A triplet can also be three notes over two beats, or over four beats, etc.) Combinations of triplets and quarter notes as in the figure above could be played as being in ¢, for example, but in ordinary tempos this measure will almost certainly be felt as a $\frac{4}{4}$ measure. Here's another combination:

In this example, I have used three different divisions of a beat in combination with quarter and half notes. It is going to be very difficult for the ear to hear this figure as anything but $\frac{4}{4}$. You should be able to see then that the more variety you put into your rhythms, the clearer the basic beat becomes. Let's look at an opposite example:

Once a beat is established, short stretches of repetitive figures like this will be heard as they are written: triplets over a basic beat, in this case. But if you carry on too long with something of this sort, the ear will start hearing something different:

 etc.

The point should be clear. If a melody is to have rhythmic "meaning" it must have rhythmic variety. As you have seen, I don't like to make flat statements that thus and such is absolutely true about music, but it is fairly safe to say that few people will go on listening very long to a melody made entirely of notes of the same length.

But there is something more than variety involved in making interesting rhythms. Very often in music you will hear two or more different rhythms going along at once. These can be called "counterrhythms":

This is certainly simple and common. For every note in one pattern there are three in the next. But counterrhythms don't have to come out quite so evenly:

In this case the two rhythms come together only at the beginning of each measure. Here is another example:

In the above, there are seven beats in one rhythm and three in the other, again coming together only at the beginning of measures. Here is still another pattern:

Here you have two rhythmic patterns which coincide only after three measures. It is theoretically possible, thus, to set almost any number and arrangements of rhythmic pulses going along at once. In actual practice, of course, composers are quite limited in what they can do. Most Western listeners can't keep track of more than three or four rhythms at once. An even more difficult problem is finding musicians who can play these odd combinations, like seven notes against four beats, for example, or eleven against five. It is like trying to rub your stomach and pat your head at the same time. You can do it, but it takes practice. Yet modern composers are more and more going in for rhythmic complications of this sort. Professional players today find that they have to learn to cope with many kinds of rhythmic difficulties that were rarely used a generation ago.

Actually, Western music is far behind that of other parts of the world in its rhythms. Over the past several hundred years European and American composers have put nearly all their effort into developing harmonies of music; rhythms have remained relatively unchanged. African musicians, for example, would dismiss a time signature like $\frac{3\frac{1}{2}}{4}$ as child's play. African music is enormously complex in its rhythms. Sometimes it will have five or six different rhythm schemes going all at once.

In any case, a great deal of our music employs counterrhythms of one kind or another, depending on the number of instruments used. But there is another point: you can make counterrhythms with one instrument alone. That is, a single melody can contain more than one rhythm:

In the example above you will hear two distinct rhythms: one on each note, and one on each group of notes. But you can create the same effect even when all the notes are the same, by the use of accents:

An accent placed on the first of each group of three notes will mark out a counterrhythm quite clearly. Obviously, by simply shifting accents around you can make all kinds of counterrhythms:

These examples of counterrhythms are quite simple. Obviously, if you can put variety into a rhythm, you can put variety into counterrhythms, too. Here I have added variety to one of the counterrhythms:

Still another way to create counterrhythms in a melody is by use of sudden changes in a pattern of melody:

The leaping notes, by suddenly departing from the melodic line as they do, are heard as if they were accented. They make quite a different pattern from the basic ¾ laid out by the clusters of eighth notes, and will be heard as a counterrhythm. Here's another way to do the same thing:

In this case the longer half notes will be heard as standing out from the melody, and will make a rhythm of their own.

In actual practice, counterrhythms are more likely to come in short spurts of two or three notes, or even for just one note. Often they are so mixed in with the basic beat that you can't single out one specific counterrhythm, but must merely say that there are countermovements in the music—places where it seems to be running against its own current for a moment, like the eddies in a stream.

One of the most common examples of this sort of counterpulse in music is syncopation. Syncopation means shifting the beginnings of a note, or a series of notes, from the strong beats to the weak beats:

Here the notes begin on the weak second and fourth beats of the measures instead of on the stronger first and third beats. In syncopation you feel a tension from the notes falling in the "wrong" place. In the second type of syncopation the notes begin on the second half of the beat:

I have put little x's to show where each beat begins. As you can see, the notes begin in different places. A syncopated figure like that one above is sometimes written like this:

And of course you can combine both types of syncopation, mixing them together anyway you wish with nonsyncopated notes. This is what happens in jazz, and to a lesser extent in rock. In jazz perhaps half of the notes are syncopated one way or another, although, of course, jazz musicians have different styles. Here's a typical jazz figure, with the x's marking the notes that begin on a beat:

Syncopated figures of this sort are not easy for beginning musicians to read. It requires special study and practice; but musicians must know how to do it, because so much music is simply crammed with syncopated figures.

Working out counterrhythms of this kind can be fascinating. Obviously, the complexities are quite enormous. If you can work one counterrhythm into a melody, why not two? Or more? And of course you can change them and shift them around, moving them backward and forward.

But there are even more complex things you can do with rhythm. Up to now I have been talking about the basic beat of music. I have used the term "basic" beat deliberately, for most music has other less important, or at least less emphatic, beats as well. Generally speaking, music has one or more secondary rhythmic pulses running along with the basic beat.

In an earlier chapter I pointed out that in a four-beat measure the first and third beats are felt to be somewhat stronger than the second and fourth beats. Taken together, these beats make up a distinct secondary rhythmic pulse:

Additionally, the first beat of a measure is felt as somewhat stronger than the others, because it is the beginning of something. So there is another rhythmic pulse. And on top of that, the experienced listener can usually hear, or "feel," longer rhythmic pulses—pulses of two or four or eight or some other number of measures, depending on the way the music is put together. Here is one possible set of secondary rhythms:

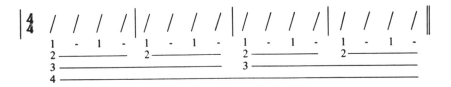

In this four-bar phrase there is the basic beat; there is a weaker rhythmic accent on the first and third beats of each measure; another secondary rhythm at the beginning of each measure; and another at the beginning of each two-bar section.

You may think that a feeling for two- or four- or eight-bar pulses is more theoretical than real, but I assure you it is not. Skilled musicians can, without counting, quite easily feel when they come to the end of a four- or eight-bar section of music (or three or nine bars, if the music is worked out that way). As a matter of fact, in the quicker tempos jazz players feel the whole twelve bars of the standard blues as one unit, and may improvise a single phrase to fit it.

And now this fact of secondary rhythms leads us into deeper

waters; for if we can have counterrhythms to the basic beat, why can't we have counterrhythms to each of the secondary beats?

We can. It works like this. Normally in 4/4 time, for example, you find a secondary pulse falling on the first and third beats of each measure, and another secondary pulse on the first beats of each measure. These secondary pulses lead us to expect phrases of music to begin on first beats, and to have their important accents on the first and third beats. And because of further secondary beats, we expect longer phrases to fit nicely over two bars, or four bars, or some other neat number. Let's look at a bit of a phrase:

The phrase of music above looks quite simple and straightforward, and that's the way you would hear it if it were played alone as it is. But in actual fact it sounds quite different if it is played like this:

It is now full of syncopation. But more important for my point, the phrase begins approximately in the middle of one measure and ends near the middle of another. The whole phrase runs counter to the secondary pulses of the music. It is, in a sense, syncopated against one or more of the secondary beats. And of course most of the notes themselves are syncopated against the basic 4/4 beat.

This practice of setting musical phrases against the secondary pulses of music has no good name. However, musicians usually use the word *phrasing* to mean approximately this, and I will adopt that word. The musical figure under discussion here is a typical example of jazz phrasing. Jazz musicians almost invariably phrase away from the basic flow of a song. In improvising, a musician will begin his phrase several beats before or after the beginnings of the sections of a song. Here is the way jazz phrasing might run against a blues pattern. The basic blues naturally divides itself into three sections, as I have done below:

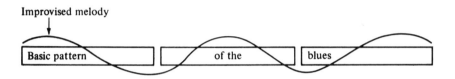

Jazz improvisers invariably phrase away from the secondary pulses of the music, but they don't all do it the same way. Various types of jazz are phrased differently, as you can easily hear if you compare, say, bop with dixieland. Rock phrasing is again different. Folk songs are phrased another way; and of course various types of classical music have their own typical phrasing patterns. Indeed, not only do types of music have characteristic sorts of phrasing, but each individual musician, from bop improviser to Baroque composer, has his own subtle way of approaching phrasing.

And so now we are led onto one more question: with musicians using counterrhythms and counterphrases everywhere, how do we know what the basic pulse is? The answer is quite simple. In any type of music where there is much syncopation or counterphrasing, there has to be a rhythm section stating the basic beat. Marching bands have drummers, jazz and rock bands have rhythm players, and so do big swing-bands. Folk singers use guitars or banjos to establish the beat. And in classical music, where there is much syncopation, some instrument is assigned to state the basic rhythms. To be sure, rhythm sections often play counter-rhythms themselves, but their main function is to keep the beat, as you will understand when you hear how often musicians complain about drummers not being able to keep metronomically accurate time. As a matter of fact, it is only because of rhythm sections that musicians today are able to play so far from the rhythmic pulses of their music. If the rhythm is not plainly stated elsewhere, the melody must stick close to the beat.

It is hardly possible in this book to go into all the different ways you can phrase and syncopate, make rhythms and counter-rhythms. It is always subtle, complicated, and personal. But I do want to make this point. The basic theories of melody and harmony which I have discussed in this book apply to almost all kinds of Western music. To be sure, one type of music emphasizes certain approaches to harmony; another goes other ways. Yet the basic principles are the same. There are jazz tunes which use exactly the same chord progression as *Old Hundredth,* and the dominant–tonic relationship is as crucial to rock as it is to Bach.

The main distinctions we feel between the various types of music we are familiar with are mostly rhythmic. Knowing what notes are in a melody, or what the chord pattern is, will not help you much in telling what kind of music it is; but tap out the rhythmic pattern of the melody with a pencil, and you can get much closer to the right answer. Rhythm is indeed the life of music.

12

The End

IF YOU HAVE WORKED your way through this book and have gotten most of it in your mind, you deserve congratulations. At this point you undoubtedly know more about music theory than many musicians, who have been too lazy to get a good understanding of their own business.

You know enough about music to write songs, make arrangements, and analyze scores of symphonies. You should have some ability to improvise, and hopefully you have developed some sense of what music is all about. But you have hardly exhausted the subject. As you go ahead you will learn about fugues and counterpoint generally, which is music with two or more melody lines running along at once. You have before you the study of atonal music, and tone rows, which were invented about fifty years ago and have had considerable effect on music. There are medieval modes, which have come back into popularity and are today much used by jazz composers, among others. There are all sorts of musics from other cultures which are worth studying, especially African music with its enormously complex rhythms, and Asian musics, which use quarter tones. The quarter tone is already beginning to show up in some of the music you normally hear, and the African rhythmic patterns have been under study, especially by jazz musicians, for years. There is the whole study of the subject of the physics of music which is still full of unknowns. Out of this study new types of musical instruments have already sprung. We will undoubtedly see much work in this direction in the future.

And then there is the whole question of the general trend music is likely to take harmonically. As you saw in an earlier chapter, harmonies have followed a natural evolution. Simple melody was followed by the use of octaves. Then 4ths and 5ths were added. And finally the system of harmonies in 3rds developed. It is obvious, with our heavy use of 6ths, 7ths, 9ths, and 11ths, that we are already using a harmonic system full of 2nds. It seems possible that the next music theory will have to take into account 2nds—be based on 2nds instead of 3rds, or at least evolve a better system for their use than we currently have. And finally, musical notation is due for a complete overhauling. Our current system makes life far more difficult for both students and professionals than is necessary.

There are more opportunities for experimentation in music than there have ever been. There is room to develop entirely new types of music, to expand the ones we have, to combine others, and to invent new ways of playing and thinking about it all. But I want to end by saying what I have said over and over again. Theory is interesting; experiments are exciting. But you must never forget that music is not black scratches on paper. . . . Music is sounds in the ear.

Exercises

Chapter One

Write out the following scales, using sharps and flats as necessary: C major; G major; A minor; E major; F minor; C♯ minor; G♭ major.

Chapter Two

Build these intervals on the following notes: a major 3rd on C; a perfect 5th on F; a major 7th on D; a minor 3rd on F♯; a diminished 5th on E♭; a minor 7th on C♯; a 6th on E; a 2nd on A; an augmented 5th on G♭; a minor 6th on F♯. What is peculiar about the last two intervals?

Chapter Three

Find the notes that belong in each of the following triads: D minor; F major; G diminished; A♭ major; C♯ minor; B♭ augmented; A major; A♯ diminished; C♭ major; B minor.

Chapter Four

Find the notes that belong in each of the following seventh chords: Dm7; B♭7; Cdim7; AM7; C♯7; D♭M7; F♯m7. Find the dominant 7ths for the following keys: C, G, E♭, B.

Chapter Five

Find which notes make a 9th, a diminished 9th, and an 11th with the following chords: Cm; A♭M; GM; Bm; G♭M; Em; FM; E♭m; F♯m; CM. Decide whether a 9th, a diminished 9th, or an 11th can be used with the following chords, and name the proper note: FM7; Em7, B♭7, GM.

Chapter Six

Write out the following inversions:

Fm in second inversion; Bm in first inversion; C7 in second inversion; B♭7 in root position; Am7 in third inversion; EM in first inversion. Write out the following chords, omitting one note: A7; B♭M; Cm7; E♭M7; Gm.

Chapter Seven

Find the dominant 7th for the following chords: GM; E♭m; Bm; FM; G♭M. Find five sets of I–IV–V chords. Find the closest two and the most distant two chords on the Circle of Fifths to the following chords: F♯M; AM, C♭M; CM, EM.

Chapter Eight

Here are three chord progressions with some blanks in them. Find chords which will fit well into the blank spaces:

| Im7 / / / | IV / / / | ? | Vm7 / / / ‖

| IM7 / / / | IV7 / / / | ? | VI7 / / / | ? | V7 / / / | IM / / / ‖

| IVM7 / / / | V / / / | ? | ♭III°7 / / / | ? ‖

Chapter Nine

Below is part of a well-known melody. Find the chord progression upon which it is built, and then write a new melody for the same chord progression.

Chapter Ten

Voice the melody you wrote for the exercise in Chapter 9 in four-part harmony.

Chapter Eleven

Rewrite your short song, freely adding syncopation and counterrhythms of your choice.

Appendix A:
Some Common Music Terms

accelerando—growing faster.
adagio—slow.
al fine—to the end.
allargando—growing broader.
allegretto—a moderately fast tempo (but slower than allegro).
allegro—fast.
andante—a moderately slow, but flowing, tempo.
adantino—a moderately slow tempo (a little faster than andante).
a tempo—at the original tempo.
calando—growing softer and slower.
cantabile—in a singing style.
crescendo—gradually louder.
diminuendo—gradually softer.
dolce—sweetly.
glissando—rapid scales produced by a sliding movement.
grave—solemn, slow.
larghetto—slowly, but faster than largo.
largo—a slow, broad tempo.
legato—smoothly.

lento—slow.

maestoso— majestically.

meno mosso—slower.

moderato—moderately.

più mosso—faster.

presto—very fast, faster than allegro.

rallentando—gradually slower.

ritardando—gradually slowing (often abbreviated *rit.*).

sordino—use mute.

sostenuto—sustained.

sotto voce—quiet, subdued.

staccato—detached, separated, abruptly disconnected.

tacet—do not play.

vivace—lively, briskly.

vivo—animated.

Appendix B:
Transposing Instruments

BECAUSE OF THE WAY music developed over hundreds of years, many instruments do not sound the notes that are written for them. This whole matter of transposing instruments is one of the things students find most confusing about music. However, anybody who wants to arrange for a band or orchestra, or even play in jam sessions, must understand the principle of transposing instruments. The idea is actually quite simple, once you grasp it.

To get the idea, consider the ordinary trumpet generally used in bands and orchestras. It is called a Bb trumpet. This means that when the trumpet player reads the C on a piece of music, the note that comes out is actually a Bb:

Written   Sounds

And in the same way, when he reads an F, the note that comes out is an Eb; when he reads a B, the note that comes out is A; and so

127

forth. In other words, the B♭ trumpet *sounds a tone below* the notes as they are written in music.

What, then, is that note in the example above called? It is written like a C, but it sounds like a B♭. Actually, either name is correct. You can call that note a "trumpet C," because C is what the trumpet player is reading. You can also call it a "concert B♭," because B♭ is what is being sounded. This term "concert" is an important one to know. A concert note or chord is the one actually being sounded, regardless of what is written. The "same as the piano" is one way of thinking of "concert."

What is the point of all this business of transposing instruments? There isn't much point. At one time it was helpful to musicians, but today it is mainly a nuisance. There is, however, one exception. Certain instruments play so high or so low that music for them would have to be written off the staff, as with this piccolo part:

Obviously it makes more sense to write such a part down an octave:

What, then, does the transposition of instruments mean to the practicing musician? Let's take the B♭ trumpet again by way of example. As a trumpet player, if you are handed the trumpet part for a piece of band music, you simply read it as written. The arranger has already transposed it into the proper key. However, suppose you pick up an ordinary piece of sheet music of a popular song, written in, say, the key of C. Because you are playing a B♭ instrument, the C's will come out as B♭'s, the F's as E♭'s, and so forth. In the end, the whole song will come out a tone lower than written—in B♭, instead of C. This presents no problem if you are playing alone; but if you are being accompanied by a piano or some other instrument whose player is reading from the same part, you will have a horrible mess.

Since your instrument is *playing a tone lower* than the music is written, you must therefore *read it a tone higher* than it is written, to compensate. That is, to have your song in C come out right, you must play it in D. Professional musicians are expected to be able to "sight-transpose" music from one key into another. It is not as hard as it sounds, but of course it takes practice. For the beginner, it is probably easier to write the song out again in the proper key.

And this, of course, is what the arranger or orchestrator does when he is working out the parts to a song. He must write parts for the transposing instruments in the proper key, so that they come out right. Another place where problems of transposing instruments come up is in jam sessions, especially in jazz, where many transposing instruments are used. If a blues in B♭ is called for, the trumpet, for example, must play a blues in trumpet C to have it come out right.

I grant that this can be confusing, but if you keep the rule in mind you can figure out what transpositions to make in any given case. The rule is this: *The key of the instrument is the note that sounds when a C is read.* Suppose, for example, you are playing a French horn in F. That means that when you read a C, the horn sounds an F. A horn player improvising a blues in F, therefore, has to play it in what he thinks of as the key of C.

There are four groups of transposing instruments, in addition to the nontransposing ones. Music written for any one of them can be used for any of the other instruments in the same group— at least as far as transposition is concerned.

Group I: The following are the common nontransposing instruments. They play in concert pitch, exactly as written. Flute, oboe, bassoon, trombone, tuba, violin, viola, 'cello, and piano. One bit of confusion: the trombone and the tuba are sometimes referred to as "Bb trombone" or "Bb tuba," because their fundamental notes are Bb. Ignore this. They are both nontransposing instruments, and play in concert pitch. In other words, this whole group of instruments can read straight off piano music, or sheet music, and come out right.

Group II: The Bb clarinet, Bb trumpet, and Bb soprano saxophone sound a tone lower than they are written. Music for them must be written in a key a tone higher than the concert key: music in F, for example, must be written in G for these instruments.

The Bb bass clarinet and Bb tenor saxophone make the same transposition, but an octave lower. Both sound whole tone plus an octave (a ninth) lower than written. This is because, although these instruments play in the lower ranges, parts for them are usually written in the treble clef. The Bb bass saxophone sounds two octaves and a tone lower than written.

Group III: The Bb alto saxophone plays a sixth lower than written. That is to say, a C comes out as an Eb. The Eb baritone saxophone plays a sixth plus an octave below what is written.

Like the tenor saxophone, it is usually written in the treble clef, although it sounds much lower. As a result, if an alto and a baritone saxophone play from the same music, the baritone will come out an octave lower than the alto.

Group IV: The English horn and the French horn sound a fifth lower than is written. In other words, they are both in the key of F. When they read a C, an F comes out. Besides the F horn, there is also in fairly common use an Eb horn. The transposition for the Eb horn is a fourth.

Group V: The piccolo plays an octave higher than music written for it. The contrabassoon and the double bass both play an octave lower than music written for them.

There are in music a number of infrequently used variations on the standard instruments which you may from time to time run across. For example, there are trumpets in both C and D, which are used primarily for the high passages in certain orchestral works, and A clarinets, although these have largely gone out of use.

Appendix C:
Ranges of the Instruments

Below is a list of the highest and lowest notes that the major instruments ordinarily play. Actually, accomplished players can extend the ranges of some of these instruments, especially the brasses. However, in arranging or orchestrating, these ranges should be kept within, unless the arranger knows that a specially trained player will be playing the part. These ranges are given in *concert pitch;* for transposing instruments they will have to be properly raised or lowered.

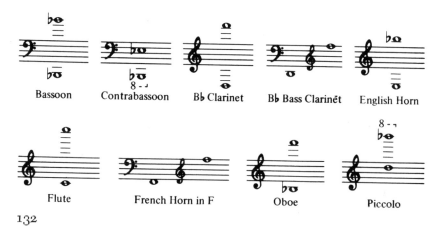

Bassoon Contrabassoon B♭ Clarinet B♭ Bass Clarinet English Horn

Flute French Horn in F Oboe Piccolo

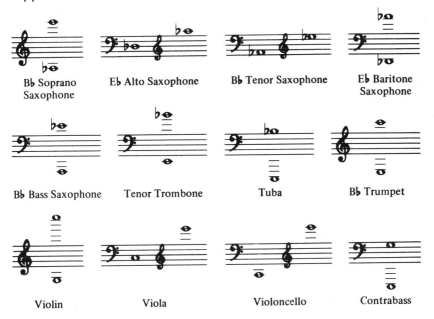

Ranges of the human voice are less exact than the ranges of instruments. The ones given in the chart below, however, are the standard ones, and should be followed in writing and arranging music unless it is known that there are singers with extended ranges. Ranges for children's soprano and alto parts are the same as soprano and mezzosoprano ranges given below.

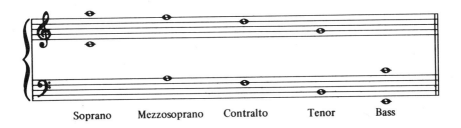

Appendix D: Basic Music Symbols

The Notes

The Notes

whole note half note quarter note

eighth note sixteenth note

The Rests

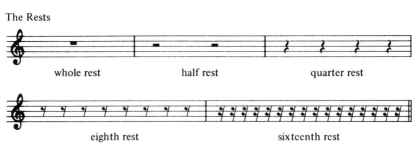

whole rest half rest quarter rest

eighth rest sixteenth rest

The Key Signatures

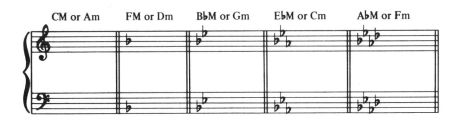

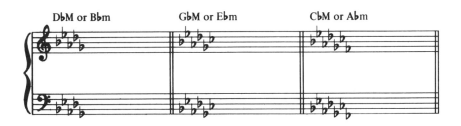

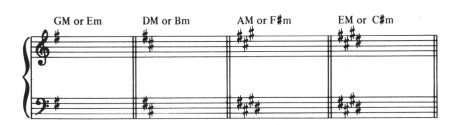

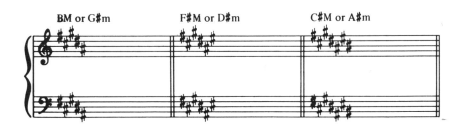

Various dynamic markings

Crescendo, cresc., ◁—grow louder.
Decrescendo, decresc., ▷ —grow softer.
Fermata, ⌒—hold note out.
Staccato, ♩ —*play note short.*
Accented note, ♩ —*attack note.*
Sforzando, sfz —forced.
Ottava, 8,8ᵛᵃ—play an octave higher than written.
Ottava bassa, 8va bassa—play an octave lower than written.
Piano, **p**—soft.
Pianissimo, **pp**—very soft.
ppp—even softer than pianissimo.
Mezzo forte, mf—moderately loud.
Forte, f—loud.
Fortissimo, ff—very loud.
fff—even louder than fortissimo.

Music often has passages which are to be played twice. In order to save trouble in writing it all out, various repeat signs are used. Unfortunately, these signs are sometimes confusing—even experienced musicians occasionally miss the repeat signs.

The simplest repeat is this: 𝄎 It means merely to repeat the previous measure. When written like this 𝄎 it means repeat the previous two measures.

When a longer passage is to be repeated, two dots are placed at the beginning and the end of the section which is to be played twice, like this:

Often, however, the composer wants the passage to end differently the second time it is played. To do this he uses first endings and second endings. They are written like this:

Another way of writing instructions for repeats uses Italian words. The words *da capo* mean "go back to the beginning." (*Capo* is the Italian word for "head.") Sometimes *da capo* is abbreviated to *D.C.* The music then may be played all the way through again. However, composers sometimes want only the beginning part of the music to be repeated. In this case they will usually write *da capo al fine* (*fine* is the Italian word for "end"). The word *fine* is written where the music is to end. In other cases the phrase *da capo al segno* is used. This means "go back to the beginning and play as far as the sign." Various signs in use are ℅ ⌀ § . Usually the sign indicates that the music jumps from that point to a final passage of music. A final passage of this sort is called a *coda*, from the Italian word for "tail," and it is normally separated from the main part of the music. *Da capo al segno* is sometimes abbreviated to *D.S.*

Appendix E:
Chord Symbols

OVER THE YEARS several different sets of chord symbols have been developed. These different symbols are still in use; even experienced players are sometimes confused as to what chord is meant. The practicing musician should know all varieties, so he can deal with any music put before him. Following are the basic symbols in general use:

Maj.—major
M—major
min.—minor
m—minor
aug.—augmented
+—augmented
− —diminished
dim.—diminished
○—diminished
∅—half diminished

Further confusion is caused by the fact that the plus sign (+) is sometimes used merely to mean "add the note following to the chord," and the minus sign sometimes means nothing at all.

Generally speaking, music publishers write chord symbols horizontally, like this: C7—9, meaning a C7 chord with the 9th added; C7—(+5), meaning a C7 with an augmented 5th; and so forth. Or they write them vertically:$C\,{}^{+9}_{7}$ meaning a C7 chord with an augmented 5th and the 9th. ${}_{+5}$

Both of these systems can be awkward to write and read. The most sensible system employs a combination of the two. In this system the symbols you have learned for the triads and seventh chords are used as a basis. Alterations to 3rds, 5ths, 6ths, and 7ths follow horizontally after the basic symbol. Added 9ths, 11ths, and 13ths—with their alterations—are placed above. This system eliminates confusion over plus and minus signs: a plus sign (+) will always mean to augment the note, a minus sign (−) will always mean to diminish it. Here then are the rules for this unified system.

The four triads are symbolized as follows:

To any triad a major or minor 7th can be added. Major 7ths are written M7. Minor 7ths are written 7.

We now have eight possible new chords:

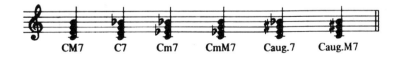

The diminished chords, however, cause us some confusion. According to this system, a written Cdim.7 ought to be a C diminished-triad to which a minor 7th has been added. However, musicians are so accustomed to thinking of this symbol to mean something else, that it is best to use the following notation for diminished chords:

To flat the fifth in any major chord, regardless of any 7th, 9th, etc., that it contains, simply place the notation −5 after the chord symbol:

Flatting the 5th in a minor chord makes it a diminished chord, and the usual symbols apply.

One problem of triads remains. It is theoretically possible to augment the 3rd, making it the same note as the 4th, and composers occasionally do so. This can be handled the way you handle alterations of the 5th, like this:

To these basic symbols now can be added any combination of major, minor, augmented, or diminished 9ths, 11ths, and 13ths, as follows:

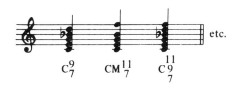

A plus or minus sign in front of the 9, 11, or 13 indicates its alteration, as follows:

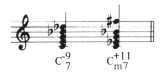

This system allows you to write in the simplest form any combination of seven notes you are likely to come across, and a good many you aren't.

Now, one last refinement. If for some reason you want to use notes a half tone apart, it can be done by adding to any 9th, 11th, or 13th an alteration of itself: 11–11, 13–13, etc. The system is now complete, for it is possible with this notation to write any combination of twelve notes you choose—which means an entire chromatic scale. Here's how such a chord might be symbolized:

$$13 - 13 + 13$$
$$11 - 11$$
$$9 - 9$$
$$\text{Cm} \ \ \text{M7}$$

Granted, at this point it would no doubt be simpler to use standard musical notation. I include this chromatic chord only to make the point that this system makes it possible to notate any combination of notes—exclusive of doublings, of course.

Index

Symbols (cont.)
minor, 40
(*see also* Nomenclature)
Syncopation, 114–115

Tempo, *see* Beats; Time
Tenors, 92, 102–103
Theory: defined, 1–14
  need for, 3
  nomenclature of, 19–23
  rules for, 75–76
  systems of, 2
  and voice-leading, 92
Time, 83–88
  cut, 107–108
  signatures, 107–108
Tonality, 15–24, 28, 33, 41–42, 86
Tone rows, 120
Tones, 6–14
  color of, 1
  emphasizing, 83–88
  half, 9
  infinity of, 9
  length of, 106–107
  non-chord, 81–83

Tones (cont.)
  passing, 83
  qualities of, 6
  relationships of, 15–19
Tonics, 42, 54, 102
  defined, 16
  rule about, 38
Transposition, 127–131
Triads, 25–36, 87
  defined, 28, 33
  development of, 91–92
  diminished, 40
  major, 49
  minor, 49
  types of, 33–35
Triplets, 109
Tritones, 96

Variety, 76, 78
Voice-leading, 57–58, 91–104
  complexity of, 92
  contrary motion in, 98
  importance of, 104
  principle of, 94–95
  rules for, 95–99